T0354907

Anathema!

America's War On Medicine

A Veteran Doctor
Offers a Cure
for What Ails
America's Health
Care System

MICHAEL PRYCE, M.D.

Order this book online at www.trafford.com
or email orders@trafford.com

Most Trafford titles are also available at major online book retailers.

Note for Librarians: A cataloguing record for this book is available from Library
and Archives Canada at www.collectionscanada.ca/amicus/index-e.html

Printed in Victoria, BC, Canada.

ISBN: 978-1-4251-8575-6 (Soft)

*We at Trafford believe that it is the responsibility of us all, as both individuals
and corporations, to make choices that are environmentally and socially sound.
You, in turn, are supporting this responsible conduct each time you purchase a
Trafford book, or make use of our publishing services. To find out how you are
helping, please visit www.trafford.com/responsiblepublishing.html*

*Our mission is to efficiently provide the world's finest, most comprehensive
book publishing service, enabling every author to experience success.
To find out how to publish your book, your way, and have it available
worldwide, visit us online at www.trafford.com*

Trafford rev. 8/19/2009

 www.trafford.com

North America & international
toll-free: 1 888 232 4444 (USA & Canada)
phone: 250 383 6864 ♦ fax: 812 355 4082 ♦ email: info@trafford.com

DEDICATION

WALT TOMALA (1960-2009)

THIS BOOK is dedicated to a great American, my patient, and a friend whose life was stripped from him too early. He was a victim of the U.S. health care system. Dedication is a commitment to a goal. It shall be my commitment to help my readers know Walt Tomala. When they all know why he forfeited his life, it should become a national commitment to change this tragic system of health care. It is for Walt Tomala that I decided to name this book, *Anathema*. I cannot think of a more fitting title to describe the outrage I felt as I watched what happened to him, and what is happening to millions of other innocent Americans like him.

TABLE OF CONTENTS

INTRODUCTION

URING MY life, I have witnessed many wars. I am not only referring to the military escapades of our federal government,
and there have been many during my lifetime, but also to the
wars on social problems. There was the war against polio, the war on
poverty, the war against drugs, the war against heart disease, the war
on breast cancer, the war on unemployment, the war on crime, and
so on. Recently, in the name of political correctness, religious fairness,
and separation of the church and state, there have been social issues,
such as the recent war on Christmas, seeking to change lifelong tradi-
tions that many Americans cherish and celebrate. Wherever one looks,
there is some segment of modern society trying to correct something,
corral something, isolate something, or destroy something that affects
Americans' lifestyles.

America's system of health care is now under attack, and very soon,
risks utter destruction.

Younger people today do not know what it was like to have access to
a doctor, and whatever the doctor ordered was done and paid for. They
know only the frustrations of trying to have their conditions treated
and having their options restricted by their insurance companies and
the federal government in the name of profit and power.

Over the course of four decades, our health care system has been
brought to its knees. Our system used to be the envy of the world, but it
has degenerated into a caste system, where the best care goes to those
who can afford it. Lately, though, even the well-to-do are struggling to
pay for their health care as this heretofore, strong foundation of our nation's infrastructure is quivering.

This is an outrage.

Recently, a war on medical care in this country is being conducted with a quiet passion that seeks an ill-fated goal. This war is generally unseen by the masses, even though they feel its effects every day of their lives. The results of the battle have entwined themselves in every facet of their being, from the cradle to the grave. Every corner of society in the US has been affected by the war, and the public has suffered for it.

Today there are an estimated forty to sixty million individuals in America without health insurance. In trying to keep up with their insurance premiums, millions of businesses are failing. Now, for the first time in history, companies are contracting with hospitals in places like India and Thailand to send patients for procedures, such as joint replacement or heart surgery, because it is cheaper to send someone to Mumbai or Bangkok for a couple of weeks than to send the employee to an American hospital for a few days. The big three automakers, the airline companies, and others are teetering on the brink of bankruptcy partly because of the high costs of health insurance premiums. The bastion of America's strength, the small business, is failing to provide health care as a benefit. America's future as an industrial giant is on the line.

THE TWO SIDES IN THE BATTLE

Over my career of nearly forty years working in medicine, I have seen a long and intense struggle for control of the health care field. Those battling to dominate it have separated into two basic camps. On one side are the health care providers, such as doctors, nurses, and allied health care professionals, as well as the sick and injured. On the other are powers that have gained control of the health care system with motivations other than the care of those sick and injured. This struggle has led to a near destruction of the time-honored and respected profession of treating the infirm.

In 1993, Hillary Clinton sought to bring government-controlled health care to the US. Prior to this, most Americans had access to a "Major Medical" insurance policy. They could go to any doctor, any hospital; they could have virtually anything done with few or no co-payments, and rarely saw the bill when treatment was completed. Mrs. Clinton wanted to replace this system with a full government-sponsored universal health care system based on the Secular Progressive European-Canadian model that would have resulted in health care rationing. Thankfully, America rejected it soundly, and her efforts were stymied by the American public.

Unfortunately, a segment of our society still feels the government should control everything. And, this group of people in politics is larger than most people realize. They are organized and well funded, and their aim is to create a Secular Progressive European/Canadian-based "universal" government program with a socialized form of health care rationing that America, as the leader of the economic world, can ill afford. This philosophy is rejected by Conservatives, who regard it as throwback to Communism, Socialism and the like. Hereafter, I shall use the term "SP" to refer to Secular Progressive and the term "EC" to represent the European/Canadian type of medical model. Combining the two yields "SPEC." The SPEC plan in Europe and Canada has resulted in basic health care, but like all government plans, the care is rationed. It does not represent what is needed or wanted in America by most Americans.

This is the very model the American people rejected soundly in the public spanking of Hillary Clinton's health care plan. Americans generally do not want socialized medicine.

Rarely does a day go by that we hear what a wonderful system the Canadians have. However, every year there is a huge migration across our northern border. Canadians are coming here to pay American doctors for services their own Canadian universal plan does not cover or are rationed to the point of desperation. This is a common theme in socialized medicine programs. Last year I treated three Canadian citizens, and Medicare even paid the entire bill for one of them.

The Canadians have a lot to lose if America institutes the SPEC plan as "national health care," as where will they all go when denied the health care in their own country? When they reach sixty-one, they will just die of coronary artery disease waiting for their rationed coronary artery bypass surgery, or the life-saving cancer procedure for which they are allocated a long waiting line.

America's "rule of law" has had its part in the destruction of our health care system and is responsible for the greatest expense in our system, that of *defensive medicine*. I am highly disturbed by how society has turned the medical errors inherent in any medical system into a lottery for lawyers to exploit; thus, sending the costs soaring for everyone. Doctors have resorted to very expensive defensive tactics to try to avoid any chance that a lawyer can turn a medical record against them in a courtroom as they seek the bounty offered by medical liability insurance.

More people work in health care than in any other industry, making it the largest business in America. According to almost everything I have read recently, health care professions are still the best bet for employment in the future. While this is fine for unemployment numbers, health care jobs do not produce goods that bring foreign money in trade back across the border.

Now, encompassing all government programs, as well as private insurance, the health care industry is at least a $2.2 trillion business, 17% of the GDP (Gross Domestic Product.) Recent predictions by the National Coalition on Health Care indicated that as the Baby Boomers enter their senior years in the next decade, the yearly cost of medicine in America would increase to $4.3 trillion, 20% of the GDP.

Three hundred million people are potential participants in the health care system. Entire industries have been spawned to make a fortune from other people's money. In many cities, the largest employer is the local hospital — a sad testament to the disappearance of American manufacturing.

With so much spent on health care every year, the overabundance of money attracts those who would exploit medicine just for the money. For any system of universal care to succeed, these economic parasites have to be eliminated.

A NEW HEALTH CARE PLAN

Even though I admit there are severe problems with our health care system, I do not want the reader to think this is just a forum for me to complain about the state of medicine in America. Many books turn out to be just exposés with no solutions. This book will be different in that I will clearly educate the reader on the roots of the War on Medicine. I hope to be able to elucidate what the problems of medicine are today and how, if they are not changed, the entire system will implode. However, I do not just end with a lot of complaining. Unlike others before me, I will present a radical plan to change the course of American health care — permanently.

It certainly can be accomplished easier than people think. Under my plan:

- Health care will be affordable.
- Health care will be sensible.
- Health care will be universal in nature without government control or interference.
- Everyone can and will be covered.
- The waste will be eliminated.

In addition, the plan is self-evolving, self-correcting and self-polic-ing: the liability problem and the scourge of repetitive medicine both suffer a deserved death. The general level of care in America will be-come affordable again and will be the envy of the world. Businesses will no longer be as likely to fail because of the punitive high costs of insurance premiums. Notice that I did not say, "high cost of health care." Workmen's compensation problems will be solved, as this model can also apply to industrial injuries. All this will allow America to take a giant step forward to being competitive in the world market again without being punished by exorbitant medical premiums that pay for meager services.

MY GOALS

If I do not succeed in anything else with this treatise, I want the reader to come away with at least one concept: insurance is a fund into which we all place our money for our protection. The only reason money should be removed from the system should be to pay for someone's needs for health care.

What has been going on, however, is that we have all been putting our money into some kind of fund and *someone else* has been taking it out. Then they restrict the care that is available so they can continue to take money out of the fund for purposes other than the health and wellbeing of those who contribute to it.

Everyone has heard the familiar denials: "We do not cover that medicine," "You cannot go to that hospital," "You cannot see that doc-tor, because he is not on our panel," "You cannot have that MRI." The myriad of denials is infuriating. The aim of this book is to educate the reader on how this has happened, how it is continuing, and how we can eliminate this theft, and develop a health care fund that results in full and complete health care for *all* the American public. I intend to in-form you about your health care system and, based on the experience of a seasoned health care professional, how to fix it for good.

The naysayer may spout this is all "too good to be true," but it only seems that way because no one has *ever* offered an alternative, afford-able comprehensive plan that has the welfare of the American people placed above all else.

The SPECs want the government to control the money, but we all know the SPEC way of doing things — raise taxes, and along with the money, the power follows. That usually ends up with the creation of a huge bureaucracy that grows only to support its own existence. On the other side, the entrepreneur wants to take all that money, because he can buy political power that keeps the money flowing. Thus, in a SPEC system, the two sides — government and entrepreneurs — work in tandem for their mutual benefit, not for the benefit of the people who need health care. None of these people cares about the health of Americans, which should be the basic aim of any health care plan.

My new plan means putting health care first. It needs to be given priority before excessive profits are removed by greedy insurance company presidents with billion dollar bonuses. Health care should supersede the motives of greedy lawyers and plaintiffs who would sink the ship for their own gain. Greedy hospital administrators, who have turned not-for-profit hospitals into megabuck businesses and whose only concern is the bottom line rather than the welfare of the sick and injured, must also come under control.

There will be critics of this book and this plan, but those who will criticize it are those who stand to have their fingers yanked out of the big pot of gold that medicine in America represents. *Only when the unnecessary players are removed and the self-interested are brought under rigid control will affordable universal health care actually become possible. Only when the SPECS are forced to admit that health care in America is not a political football will real reform be possible. Only when liability costs are controlled will the public enjoy true complete access to health care.*

Total health care in the past was — and can still be — affordable, but it can only be a reality if it is controlled by those who put health care first and profit last, and government interference is taken out of the picture.

If health care is mismanaged in the next five years, America could end up as a second-rate or, worse, a third-rate world power. If the country falls into the hands of the SPECs, health care, as we have known it, will simply dissolve into a regulatory fog of oblivion, and we will be relegated to a SPEC-type existence with high taxes and health care rationing.

This is bad news for Baby Boomers as they enter the final quarter of their lives. Every American needs to shout, "Over my dead body!" If not, America will cease to be the country we know and love. This issue is so critical that we can no longer bury our heads in the sand.

The reader might ask why an individual like me chooses to speak up. The answer is very simple. I am a Baby Boomer. I was born just after World War II. My generation experienced the best of everything, and I have had a good life. However, as I enter the last quarter of my life, I have come to realize that the most important part of life, the part I would most like to be guaranteed, is about to be stripped from my grasp. I am referring to the ability to get good, affordable health care in my senior years.

I do not have national name recognition like some who write, but I have had the privilege of being involved in the health care of my fellow countrymen for almost forty years. My advantage is that I have been very observant over those years. I have witnessed the sad downhill slide of our nation's health care system. Over the years, I have done my part to try to right some of the wrongs, but as an individual what I could achieve has been limited. Now I do not feel I can keep quiet any longer.

When I have finished, I want every American to have the understanding and the means to correct the problems with the American health care system. Then I want them to do something about it. When they see the CEO of United Health Care take a $1.74 billion bonus while their premiums go through the roof, their services decline, and their doctor gets run out of business, I want them to do something about it. The health care plan herein will offer a tool to exorcise these financial demons and put health care, as a financial and social worry behind us forever.

In the following pages, a solution in the way of a radical new health care program will be introduced that will guarantee that Americans can enjoy and afford their health care in the future. I feel the program presented in this book will actually be a program that Americans can wrap their arms around and which they will demand be implemented.

So, as you read this book, keep in the back of your mind that this problem is the single largest and most important matter that America faces today. It exceeds energy problems, environmental problems, foreign policy entanglements. It even supersedes the question of who is president, for without adequate and affordable health care, every institution in our country will eventually topple.

I hope this book will enlighten you to the effects of this war. I hope you will use its principles to redirect the energy where it belongs and end this war on health care. You have the power to put America on the right track before a true disaster for all time occurs. Luckily, America still has options.

Sit back and look at the plan that a health care professional envisions after being in the system for nearly forty years. Once you have finished, I will wager you will accept the health care plan that is presented and demand it be implemented.

Part One:

THE ROOTS OF THE PROBLEM

I will start by examining what happened over the past forty years that led to the current horrendous situation of healthcare in America.

Chapter One

THE DESTRUCTION OF THE AMERICAN HEALTH CARE SYSTEM

A COLLEAGUE OF mine, who has asked to remain unnamed for fear of government reprisals, is a former professor of anesthesia at a major university. He served as a member of a committee at the Health and Human Services Department in 1970. He was present when the chairman of the committee, who seemed angry and smug throughout the meeting, made a stunning statement that reverberates even today. He stated, "The problem with medical care is that the doctors have all the money and that is going to change."

In my estimation, that statement by a government official — that the people who provide the care are somehow overpaid and do not deserve what they are paid for their work — was the opening shot in America's War on Medical Care. In the profession of plumbing, for instance, the plumbers have all the money. Why has there not been such a power move on the profession of plumbing? We still have plumbers who can tailor their construction to the needs of the homeowner. They are expensive. Why is there no attack on plumbers?

America has made some unbelievable blunders in her short history, and this attack on medical care has to rank near the top. Four decades ago, America had undisputedly the best health care in the world, but the decision that doctors made too much money was a misguided perception. In 1970, people had cheap health care *and* they had access to doctors. Today, that access is threatened severely, and the cost is utterly embarrassing. Doctors certainly do not have all the money as is witnessed by doctors being forced out of medical practice in great numbers.

WHY ATTACK MEDICAL CARE?

For four decades now, a war has been raging on medical care in America. It is an odd war. Usually, wars are fought over territory, religion, money, ethnic hatred, and the like. Why has there been such a campaign against medical care? It seems strange that anyone would want to attack a system that provided such a grand service to mankind. However, it did begin, and it continues today. I believe it came about, as separate forces, each with their own problems and agendas, successfully conducted a multi-front attack on the providers of health care in America.

Part of the problem is that Americans were allowed to slip into the comfort zone of a health care system that literally covered everything, and the consumer never saw the bill. It became an ipso facto right of American citizenship to have "free" health care. The major medical policy literally covered anything and everything doctors ordered. People could go to any doctor and any hospital, where they could literally have anything done. They had full drug coverage, and it was all paid for. It was utopia for Americans on the private side. On the public side, Medicare and Medicaid took care of the elderly and the indigent. Although there were some limitations, they basically had the same coverage, except for drugs. For the most part, people were not burdened with deductibles, and co-pays had not yet been implemented in great numbers.

While Americans were considered to have the best health care in the world, the Europeans opted for socialism. They designed and enacted government-controlled-and-paid-for health care that had rationing — a distasteful concept to Americans — built in. The European model, however, became the model that many political types in this country sought to copy in the US.

Doctors were not held in as high esteem in Europe as they were in the US. The amalgamation of thought that carried over from Marxist thinking included the concept that doctors had to be brought down socially and financially to the same level as the common worker. Communist thinking held that one of the last barriers to control the Western governments was the position of the physician in Western Civilization. The one big stepping-stone to be overcome in America was for the Secular Progressive movement to bring medical care to its knees so that it could be taken over. After that, the goal was total government control of virtually everything.

However, the war started on medical care had to be carefully plotted because Americans would not give up their health care easily. The Clintons found that out in the early 1990s when they tried in vain to convert our system of medical care to a SPEC-type of total government-controlled socialized health care. Americans just did not want that type of health care, and Congress overwhelmingly rejected their health care plan.

Americans still do not want that type of health care, but the war has taken its toll. Americans are so put upon by the complexities of just getting to see a doctor when they are sick and how to pay for it, that they are ready for just about anything. A recent poll indicated that 69% of American citizens were in favor of a universal health care system. This is the first time I am aware of that the majority of Americans indicated they were so sick of the health care system that they would rather the government take it over.

Therefore, for a period of nearly four decades, medical care and the medical profession have been under a steady attack. The adversaries of, what was once the best health care system in the world, came from the ranks of the government, insurance companies, hospital administrators, and the legal profession. Each of these anti-medical care combatants had motive and method.

The population in general did not take part in this war. Instead, they were relegated to spectators to the war, pushed around by those who controlled the purse strings. They were given no choices in the matter, even though they began to shoulder more and more of the cost.

These relentless attacks have now left us with a health care system that is much changed. We vacated a dignified, professional system that was comparatively inexpensive, personal and innovative, where care could be customized to the individual needs of each patient who had freedom to choose a doctor or hospital. The system featured a sensitive touch from a familiar doctor who was attentive to the needs of his patient. There were very few deaths from medical mistakes. What more could we ask for from a health care system?

WHAT HAPPENED?

About 1970, a great information explosion occurred in medicine. Treatments for diseases that had been considered terminal or untreatable were beginning to fall under the control of doctors. People were living longer and healthier lives. Health care spending for the entire nation in 1970 totaled $75 billion, which represented a mere $356 per person. By 2006, however, health care spending had risen to over $2 trillion. This comes to a total of $6,697 (in inflation-adjusted dollars) per person. Thus, we now have a health care system that is nearly *twenty times as expensive* as it was in 1970.

Despite this fact, a huge section of our population goes without access to medical care or without the ability to pay the high costs. However, the high costs of medicine are not equating into doctors becoming millionaires, such as the media and government would have people believe — far from it. Epidemiological studies indicate that a primary care physician in a solo or small group practice in America today will make 25% less than a hairdresser. This disparity in income occurs after the physician spends fifteen hard years of study while the hairdresser barely needs a year of training and a pair of scissors. Therefore, the money is not flowing to the doctors.

There are hidden costs in that total of $6,697 per person that do not necessarily pertain to the strict care of sick and injured Americans. This hidden expenditure includes all costs of basic and specialty care, defensive medicine, repetitive medicine, entrepreneurial medicine, fraud and abuse, CEO and executive bonuses, and the ridiculous rise in health care premiums with reduced services attached. It also includes the costs of Medicare and Medicaid, with the inherent costs of the bureaucracy that subtracts valuable funds, as the CMS (the Center for Medicare Services) tries to enforce their regulations.

In spite of the costs, people are having increasing difficulty accessing their physicians of choice, and this is no longer just a problem of the indigent, poor, or those on Medicaid. Virtually everyone has trouble getting a timely appointment to see a doctor.

Along with that, health care providers are now among the most heavily regulated individuals in the country. They are no longer able to provide individualized care customized to the needs of each patient. Generally, patients can no longer choose their doctor and frequently cannot choose which hospital to use. The result is that they are often forced to drive long distances because their health care plan will not pay the bill at their hospital of choice. The heart of the system, the solo or small group practitioner, is nearly extinct. They have been replaced by large impersonal groups, managed care groups, or worse yet, hospital-based physician employees. They have fallen under the thumb of aggressive hospital administrators, intent on running a hospital like a Fortune 500 company.

In short, what we have metamorphosed to is a system that is very un-American in nature, one that hardly provides the best health care in the world. Our very American style of medical practice has been crushed by powerful well-organized forces, whose sole intent is to take control of the patient's health care away from the health care provider and strip the dollars away in profits.

WHAT IS HAPPENING NOW?

In a 2007 speech to the Cleveland City Club, President Bush stated, "People *have* access to health care. After all, you just have to go to the Emergency Room."

If ever in my life I have heard a shortsighted, ill-informed remark, this has to be it. For the President of the US to suggest that everyone who cannot get a timely appointment with a doctor simply visit the Emergency Room and utilize the safety net for medical care is just plain ignorant and shocking. But the sad fact is that is exactly what is happening. Sadly, our out of touch Congressional leaders have the same shortsighted impressions for many reasons, which we will explore.

In the same breath, Bush made the statement that, "America has the best health care in the world." As we will soon see, he is very wrong on that count.

He went on to say that, "the objective has got to be to make sure America is the best place in the world to get health care; that we're the most innovative country; that we encourage doctors to stay in practice; that we are robust in the funding of research and that patients get good quality care at a reasonable cost."

Once again, our President was sadly mistaken. All indications are to the contrary. As we shall soon see, a study just reported in December 2008 by the National Physicians Foundation indicates that, within the next two years, as many as 54% of all American primary care doctors intend to quit the profession and retire, or simply seek areas of medicine where they no longer have patient contact because they are fed up. This is a huge crisis brewing with unimaginable and disastrous consequences for an already burdened and failing health care system. Just as Nero fiddled while Rome burned, President Bush, President Obama, and the American Congress stood silent and allowed the banking industry, home mortgage industry, the auto industry, countless others, and finally, health care in America to decline into bankruptcy and failure on their watch.

What defines a "reasonable cost" when doctors are being paid so poorly they have to give up their practice and go out of business, retire, or become employees of a hospital? Because of the War on Medical

Care, health costs have not remained reasonable. In spite of the rape of doctor's fees and the usurpation of the doctors' control of the care of their patients, medical care in the US has become monumentally more expensive than in most other industrialized nations. In fact, our system is twice as expensive as our next closest nation, Switzerland as reported by Voice of America News in 2006. As expensive as it is, we have unbelievably fewer services.

Sadly, some in our government have adopted the same fallacious thinking as the socialists who were responsible for the imposition of the SPEC system in Europe and Canada. Their thinking is that government control of health care by non-medical bureaucrats can provide acceptable health care. This micromanagement has left us with a fragmented and discordant medical system that costs nearly twenty times as much as it used to; a system in which it is estimated that over a hundred thousand people die of medical mistakes each year.

Our Congressional leaders are also not without blame or shame. This destruction of such a fine institution shows a lack of caring or understanding by our political leaders. They have their own health care plans free from the myriad of problems that the American public lives with every day.

HOW CAN BUREAUCRATS IN A DISTANT CITY MAKE WISE DECISIONS FOR US?

During the Vietnam War, I was a member of the US Navy. While I was home on leave, I ran into a friend of mine who was just redeployed out of the war after his required time "in country." He was a Marine in Vietnam, and I was in Naval Intelligence in Europe during the Cold War. He revealed some astounding things that have a curious parallel to the War on Medical Care.

The restrictions on his ability to fight were unconscionable. Civilians were micromanaging the war from desks in Washington. At times, he and his friends in arms were limited to only one cartridge per person, and had *no ammunition* in their rifles when not under fire. At his last firebase, they were separated from the ammunition in the base armory by over six hundred yards of open ground, so if an attack happened, they had to run across this open ground to get to the ammunition while the bullets were flying. Their ability to direct the management of a firefight on the ground in Vietnam was usurped by someone sitting behind a desk in Washington, frequently with no knowledge of how to conduct such an operation.

The parallels between their war and the War on Medical Care are amazing. In both cases, the people actually tasked with doing the duty were hamstrung by their own government.

The motivation behind this is puzzling to me. Somewhere in the period from the late 1960s to the early 1970s, a philosophy developed that the government ultimately knows better how to manage highly professional services than the people who are trained to conduct them. Nevertheless, after the experience of the war in Vietnam, which we lost, why would someone want to destroy a health care system that had been working so well using the same mentality that we used to lose that war? Is it the same philosophy that President Clinton demonstrated when asked on CBS's "60 Minutes" why he dared to have a sexual relationship with a twenty-one-year-old White House Intern just two feet from the Oval Office? He answered, "Because I could."

Is that why we are in the trouble with health care today — because someone "could"? That is not the representative government we all covet so highly. Rather, it smacks of Soviet policy and Politburo control.

WE HAVE FOUND THE ENEMY AND IT IS OUR GOVERNMENT!

Sadly, it was our own government, which initiated the War on Medical Care. The motivation was not necessarily so some government type could wrest the money from the doctors — that was the side effect. Like the Vietnam War, the motivation was *power*. The actual drive by third party payers, whether government controllers or private insurance companies, was to force our doctors into "managed care" organizations heavily controlled by government officials and insurance company boards with no knowledge of what was right for the patient. In doing so, they destroyed the beauty of the medical care system that existed in our country.

If the study conducted by the National Physicians Foundation is correct in predicting the coming holocaust, America is going to be left with only catastrophic health care. While we have problems, this is still America, and no one, not even the government, can force a person to practice medicine while impossible constraints are placed upon their efforts and their income. While some kind of Taft-Hartley-type legislation could force an immediate return to the workplace, no one can force people to work if they simply quit, and all indications are that that is about to happen in record numbers. Furthermore, America is soon to learn the lesson that if one is forced to charge less than it costs them to run their business, the business eventually collapses. That day has arrived.

American citizens and the government alike can ill afford to take this survey lightly. I am one of those physicians who are actually facing professional extinction, and I, like many of my colleagues, have simply "had it."

As with all services, it is true that there were some problems in our health care system. However, the response to those problems has over-shot the goal of containing those who would purposely defraud the system or who were simply inept. This knee-jerk overreaction by con-trollers of government entitlement programs and insurance companies by changing the basic practice model of our doctors had the effect of destroying the system that brought the world's best health care to all Americans. This is a real life version of "throwing the baby out with the bath water."

But why would our government officials, who are elected by the people to serve them, want to give more power to unelected bureau-crats? The reason was simple. Medicare was started as "an assist pro-gram" for seniors. It was never meant to be a full-service program, but the AMA (American Medical Association) lobbied hard for the govern-ment to make it so. Once they did so, there was not enough money to make it work, resulting in a huge $60 billion shortfall. President Nixon declared it a financial crisis and legislation was enacted to bring the project under control. That was about the time when Congress (with Nixon's approval) broke into the Social Security Administration Trust Fund. That is also when they came up with the model to allow doctors to treat patients, and then they would go back, audit them, and recoup more funds than they actually paid the doctors (more on this in the chapter on entitlements).

These government types who never see patients have the mistaken idea that they can better make the call on individual health care deci-sions as to what is "reasonable and necessary" than those with at least fifteen years of training beyond high school and years of experience in the field of medicine.

HOW THE WAR IS BEING FOUGHT
Before the government became heavily involved, the very heart of our medical care system was the small group and solo practitioner, the very person who was most attentive to the needs of the individual patients, the one who knew them the best. Then government programs killed

the intimate doctor-patient relationship. People lost the one aspect of medical care — access to the one person who was innovative and could tailor medical care to the individual needs of the patient — that made us the best in the world.

There is a reason why doctors have not been able to keep control of their profession: the government has systematically cordoned doctors off from the public with federal regulation. This onerous system replaces the attentive care to the needs of the patient with one in which health care personnel mandatorily have to worry more about what is *documented* than what is *done*. This shifting of priorities has become monumentally expensive, as the government has created so many regulations that they conflict with one another, and, as health care workers toil to try to stay within the regulations, they spend overwhelming amounts of time and money unnecessarily. In addition, the government (that is, *we the people*) cannot afford to pay for this. As evidence for this fact, one only needs to realize that predictions are running rampant that Medicare will run out of money by 2017. Robert Pear has reported in the New York Times that the recession is draining funds so quickly that if present trends continue, Medicare will be out of money by the year 2017 (http://beltwayblips.dailyradar.com/stories/System_Failures. 2009.

Doctors are so pinned down by Medicare regulations that they simply are not able to act. All the laws of due process have been abrogated with respect to doctors working in the Medicare program. Inadvertent fraud by physicians without intent is, for the most part, the rule. The Medicare regulations are so many, so complex, and so confusing that the doctors simply do not know which ones to follow. The penalties and punishments of doctors for inadvertently violating the mess of Medicare regulations go completely against the American philosophy of "innocent until proven guilty."

In addition, the billing systems that overwhelm most doctors were actually set up with specific purposes in mind: first to confuse the doctor-purveyors of small business, who have virtually no real business sense; then the model acts to underpay the doctors for their services. Then the plan is to go back and recoup those payments from the doctors with penalties and interest tacked on because of violations that were most likely unintentional.

One can draw a simple inference as to why this is happening: Medicare could not pay the costs of health care, so the government relied on the old assumption that doctors were rich, and that government bureaucrats could perform audits and catch the physicians in the web of confusing regulations. This would initiate fines, penalties, and interest payments that would cause the doctors to pay back many more dollars than they were initially paid. This should help explain the statement that was mentioned above that, "the trouble with medicine in America is the doctors have all the money." While this once might have been true, clearly it no longer is. Attempts to implement this way of funding government programs will result in trying to recoup money from people who are not as wealthy as thought. It will literally run most doctors out of business!

Instead of enlisting the doctors' help in setting standards of care and payment schedules for certain services, they allowed them to treat, bill, and then be subjected to a protocol that can result in the doctor ending up in violation if he overcharges *or* undercharges for the service, depending upon the codes he uses. Either way, he could be found in violation and end up paying back to the government more than he was paid.

In any other system in America, if a bill is discovered to be mistaken — either inflated or undercharged — it is adjusted. The government way is to make the doctor pay back *all* the money, then tack on interest and penalties. In 1986, the Congress passed a law that allowed the damages to be *tripled*. The doctor is not even allowed to keep the fee that he should have received. If he cannot pay the fines, the government can take any possession, such as cars, buildings, or equipment (just as the DEA does with illegal drug dealers) to gather valuables in trade for the mistaken billings. What good is it for the government to have all these possessions if they run the doctors out of business?

We will all bear witness to this war on medicine as the government RAC's program (Recovery Audit Contractors) begins its audits in 2009. The Physicians Foundation study predicts 54% will leave practice anyway. What will happen to the 46% left behind in the financial blitzkrieg? It will be interesting to watch. If one thinks the recent financial and mortgage crisis has been bad, just watch what happens as medicine in America draws her last breath.

Not only is the above true, but the way a doctor can be investigated is nothing short of shocking. There are few understandable standards by which Medicare says what something should cost, or what treatment or procedure should be allowed. The newly concocted "E & M" (Evaluation and Management) rules force a "one size fits all" system onto the basic unit of medicine for all doctors — the history and physical. The entire system of audits is all based on what the doctor documents in his chart.

The investigator could cite the doctor in several ways, mostly based on his assumption that the service was not "reasonable and necessary." The level of service could be questioned, but no standard says what service reaches what level of significance, and thus, receives higher or lower reimbursement; the physician is left to guess what level the service might pass.

DETAINEES IN GUANTANAMO HAVE MORE RIGHTS THAN AMERICAN DOCTORS DO

When the investigator comes in, he could say the physician over-billed or under-billed, and the doctor could be cited either way. Medicare can then decide to estimate the percentage of his practice that the service constituted and multiply the penalties based on that percentage. The next step is to levy a fine on the doctor, and if he does not or cannot pay immediately, then fines, penalties, and interest accumulate. It is not like when someone steals government money in a fraud scheme. When doctors are involved, these financial penalties are levied without regard to due process or a court proceeding. In addition, under the False Claims Act of 1986, the damages are now tripled.

The doctor can profess his innocence but the fines have to be paid before he gets his "day in court." However, he does not even get to go to court!. He has to have "hearings" in the different departments of the CMS (Center for Medicare Services), the Health and Human Services, Justice Department, and the like. The appeals process can go on for as much as twenty years, with the fines, penalties, and interest accumulating during the time the process goes on.

If the doctor does not pay, the government can confiscate any equipment he used in the course of his "violation," including the building he practices in, furniture, computers, plus any equipment, such as X-ray machines, EKG machines, medicines in his office — all before a court says he is actually guilty. If it wants to, the government can carry the appeals process out until the doctor dies without ever having a jury decide if he is actually guilty. If we were to compare this system to a murder complaint, this would equate to the government executing the suspect before a trial occurs, only to find out later that he was not guilty. The trick is to use the word "fraud," making the public scorn the doctor for his acts.

These RAC's audits have the potential of labeling *every doctor in*

America a crook. Once the audits start, virtually every doctor could be guilty of "fraud," and the public is likely to take a closer look at what is going on.

During the process, the doctor will need the advice of legal counsel, but while the government can limit what the doctor is reimbursed for his services, the government puts no restriction on what an attorney can charge him for his defense of the same. Therein lays the heart of the war on medicine.

So, even if the doctor is actually innocent of the charge, most doctors will just pay the fine because exhausting the possible appeals could cost hundreds of thousands of dollars in legal fees.

Somewhere in all of this, I think the spirit of the constitutional right of citizens of the US for due process and against undue seizure of property by the government has been lost. The detainees in Guantanamo, Cuba have more rights to protest their innocence than American doctors do.

There is a war against medicine in this country, but like all wars, it could become very unpopular very quickly with negative results for those who perpetrate it. Americans are upset at the inability to get a timely appointment with a doctor now.

Americans have an innate ability to understand that not everyone can be guilty of a crime; they also have a history of what to do with a bad law. The King of England found that out when citizens in Boston tossed his tea shipments into Boston Harbor.

The coming confrontation will be interesting. I have patients apologizing to me for the pitiful reimbursements they see when they get their EOB or the bill they see when Medicare pays me. It will be interesting to see the public's response when they see their doctors named in fraud litigation while they realize the reimbursement for services by their doctor are already at an embarrassingly low level. It is one thing to pay a doctor a miniscule amount for what his education, time, and experience are worth, but then to call him a crook is shameful.

SO WHY STAY IN AND PARTICIPATE IN THE MEDICARE PROGRAM?

Why any doctor decides to stay in the Medicare program (or medical practice at all for that matter) today is puzzling. In reality, doctors have stayed in because seniors need health care. The financial punishment doctors receive for this honorable service is disgraceful and un-American. However, news of over 600,000 audits aimed at doctors to make up for present shortfalls in funding could cause a revolt.

The CMS has to be careful about how they handle this problem. The one thing doctors have failed to recognize is that the most powerful weapon they have in dealing with controlling agencies is the power to withhold their services. Just recently, a news flash came to the office fax machine announcing that Medicare will check and see if a Medicare recipient is delinquent on their federal taxes, and that Medicare will withhold that recipient's payments to the doctor until the tax deficit is settled. If I understand this fax correctly, that means the money for the doctor's fees will go to satisfy the delinquent tax bill, so the doctors' reward is now to be responsible for paying the income tax for those who do not pay their taxes. This program called the Federal Payment Levy Program is meant to withhold Medicare payments to Medicare providers who are delinquent on their taxes. If a doctor treats a nurse, physical therapist or some other provider, the government can withhold payments to health care providers until the tax issue is settled. As reported within, the CMS has indicated they will continue to cut, cut, cut doctors fees until sufficient doctors drop off the program. If they continue this bravado, they could end up with a lot of failed medical practices or a country full of angry physicians who could literally bring the program to a halt.

In addition, America is now aging and needs more doctors with specialized training in the care of elderly patients. In the Annual Review of Gerontologists and Geriatrics, Volume 25, 2005 reported in Chapter 7 it was indicated that there are only around seven thousand gerontologists in the country. After the first wave of Baby Boomers enters the program, there will be a need for an additional thirty-six thousand Gerontologists. However, young doctors are very tuned into Medicare pay schedules and they know that gerontologists are some of the lowest paid of all doctors. In addition, the majority of their patients are Medicare-based and that is the lowest pay scale on the books. There is also the myriad of Medicare rules and regulations that are, in my estimation, responsible for the threatened exodus of doctors, as reported by the National Physicians Foundation. Is it any wonder that geriatric medicine is one of the most unpopular fields of practice?

These overkill responses are aimed at the very few people who take advantage of the program. Government estimates are that there is between $60 and $70 billion in purposeful fraud operations in the country each year. It is clear to me, as an alumnus of the FBI Citizens Academy, that the vast majority of fraud is conducted by people and companies who set out to purposefully defraud the government. They are generally pharmaceutical operations or large operations with durable medical products. This fraud exists only because of the government's interference in health care as people realize the unbelievable loopholes that exist in the Medicare program. Of the $60 to $70 billion lost to fraud each year, only $1.6 billion is recovered through efforts of the FBI and other government agencies, yet the government seems intent on trying to fund its failing Medicare program on the backs of already strapped physicians.

IT IS NOT WORKING AND IT NEEDS TO CHANGE.

It is evident the government program is not working in many aspects. The government does a great job as a cash flow organization, but its ability to manage something as complex as medical care has proven to be suspect. The time is ripe to replace the system *before* it implodes financially with one that restores the control of the practice of medicine to those who know it best.

Every study done in the past fifteen years has indicated that people prefer the control of their health care be in the hands of the doctors. If this is true, then why does Congress not acquiesce to the demands of the electorate? Why do they ignore the voters? More than anything else, to preserve what is good in our system and return us to the ranks of the best health care in the world, the direction our medical system is taking needs to change.

Chapter Two

THE ROLE OF HEALTH INSURANCE COMPANIES

WHILE THE government has been waging war on medical care providers, others have been busy too. Reinforcements in the war have come from insurance companies.

THE INSURANCE COMPANIES STAGED A COUP D'ÉTAT OF MEDICAL CARE IN AMERICA

For decades, insurance company executives had been agonizing over the fact that doctors were cost shifting what they were losing on the government side to the private side. Insurance companies tried many tactics to gain control of the costs, but providers were always one step ahead of them.

To deal with the problem, insurance company conglomerates formed management groups, with the sole purpose of overhauling the traditional form of compensation to providers. One such group was the "Jackson Hole Group," so-called because it held a secret meeting in the early 1990s in Jackson Hole, Wyoming to discuss the problem. The common feeling amongst the attendees of the meeting was that there was only so much time left until the system collapsed. From this meeting changes came that affected the future of health care in America.

One reason that they were in a rush to make the change was that they had the perception that time was running out on the health insurance industry, and that the medical system would go bankrupt in ten to twenty years. An additional goal was to make as much money as they could before political forces took over and socialized the health care system.

As told to me by a former high-ranking insurance official who attended the meeting, the basic goal of the plan that the attendees came up with was to remove providers from control of the process.

Out of that meeting came a common business plan adopted by the major insurance companies that was virtually copied by every other insurance company. The name of this scheme was "Managed Care," and it was the coup d'état of medical care in America. The HMO (Health Maintenance Organization was born and America was changed radically.

This plan initially had merit. It was to be a cooperative between the insurance companies, health care providers, and the government. They had great plans to include the doctors in helping to set up care plans that would benefit both sides, but they quickly realized that they could not control the liability costs. Defensive medicine tactics by doctors had become so expensive that the Jackson Hole Group advised a change in strategy.

Once the decision to change their plans for a cooperative effort was made, they opted to try to make as much money as possible, and it metamorphosed into a system better referred to as "Managed Denial." Under so-called "Managed Care," decisions over medical care were taken away from doctors in favor of keeping medical treatments, procedures, and supplies at minimum so insurance companies could make huge profits. Therefore, a model that originally sounded good and had merit has kept changing in favor of higher and higher premiums, fewer and fewer services to the patients, and bottom-of-the-barrel payments to health care providers.

AMERICANS ARE SUFFERING FROM THE AMERICAN HEALTH CARE SYSTEM

Americans are suffering from this, and we are the laughing stock of the world, as statistics pour out every year showing the unbelievably poor showing of the richest country in the world with regard to the quality and cost of health care. A survey by the AFL-CIO with its affiliate Working America conducted from January 2008 to March 2008 and involved 26,500 people is the largest opinion poll available on health care. It revealed some interesting facts about the American public, most of which were insured, educated, and employed:

- One-third of all families opted out of medical care because of the high cost to them even after they paid exorbitant premiums.
- One-fourth of those families reported problems paying for the

care they really needed.

- More than half of the insured reported that their insurance does not cover the care they need at an affordable price.
- Forty-six percent reported spending between $1000 and $5000 out-of-pocket on health care in the previous year, even with an insurance policy in place.
- Seventeen percent reported that they spent in excess of $5000 in out-of-pocket costs, even with an insurance policy in place.
- One-third of all college graduates indicated that they avoided health care because of the cost.
- Nearly fifty percent reported they or a family member held on to a job just to try to retain health care benefits, even as bad as they were.
- Over 80% indicated that their families "have just enough to get by or are falling behind."
- A large percentage of Medicare enrollees stated that their prescriptions are just not covered or are simply unaffordable.
- Ninety-five percent of everyone surveyed indicated they are "somewhat" or "very concerned" about the inability to afford health care in the future.

EMPLOYERS ARE SUFFERING TOO

Employers have also suffered through the largest raise of premiums in this nation's history. There is no alternative solution to their problem of paying for the health care of their employees, and thus, employers have been forced to pay higher and higher premiums for skimpy skeleton-like health care policies.

One recent survey, reported at ExpansionManagement.com indicated that "89% of 1400 chief financial officers ranked health care including escalating costs for employee health plans as their biggest concern, easily topping energy costs, the federal budget deficit, government spending and other issues."

Information being passed around the insurance industry earlier this decade indicated stormy weather ahead for employers. One particular lecture utilized data taken from a Kaiser/HRET Survey of Employer-Sponsored Health Plans in 2003 and a Bureau of Labor Statistics 2003 National Compensation Survey. Those studies provided the initial amount employers contributed and the percent of contribution. To clarify, the lecturer, not Kaiser/HRET, indicated a projection of the wages earned by a family of four with two working parents and two children from 2003 to 2021. The wages were compared with health benefits as a percentage of total compensation for the family with a 4.6% annual growth rate in household income and the projected 12% annual growth rate in health insurance premiums. It indicated that in 2003, the average wage earned by a family of four with two working parents was $48,333, of which 19% of the income provided by the employer went to health care. Prior to the recent mortgage crisis, a lending institution generally would not lend a family any more money for a thirty-year mortgage on their home's monthly payments than 25% of their total income. In 2003, the average family was already spending nearly one-fifth of their income for health care premiums. This hints at how much the system has degenerated into a profit-based system since 1970, when we were only spending $356 per person per year on health care.

This ominous presentation of the future illustrated the dangerous path we are on as a nation. If those 2003 projected trends were to come true, in the year 2021, the same average family income was projected to be $108,423 of which 63% *would go to health benefits*. So, from 2003 to 2021, employers would be responsible for paying for an increase from $6,620 to $49,843 if health insurance continues to be a benefit.

In 2003, the insurance industry projected that a watermark existed right in the middle, at the year 2010. That is when employers were predicted to reach the funding breaking point and *could no longer afford to offer health insurance as a benefit*. In fact, in 2007, we already began to see small businesses drop health insurance in great numbers as a benefit.

If employers are no longer able to afford this rate of growth, how can the federal government expect to absorb this catastrophic burden without huge controls on the insurance industry or massive taxes? The only way it can be done is with the extreme health care rationing characteristics of all SPEC-type government health care programs.

Here are a few other statistics and projections, including some potentially conflicting projections by national experts:

- Health care spending of $1.9 trillion in 2005 consumed 15.5% of the economy, up sharply from 13.2% in 2000. Health spending in 2005 was nearly double that of education, and 3.6 times defense spending. (Health Reform Program, Boston University School of Public Health, 2/05)
- According to the October 2006 "Health Care in America" survey, Americans are increasingly uneasy about high health care costs and are uncertain of their families' ability to afford health insurance. (Telephone survey of 1,201 Americans conducted in

September by the Henry J. Kaiser Foundation, ABC News, and *USA Today*.) Eighty percent of respondents said they were dis-satisfied with the total cost of health care in the US, which is expected to hit $2.2 trillion in 2006 (and double that, to $4.7 tril-lion in the next decade). Underscoring America's sense of un-ease, the survey found that six in ten Americans with insurance are worried about their ability to afford coverage over the next five years.

- Premiums for employer-sponsored health coverage raised an av-erage 7.7% in 2006, less than the 9.2% increase recorded in 2005 and the recent peak of 13.9% in 2003. This year's survey recorded the slowest rate of premium growth since 2000, though premi-ums still increased more than twice as fast as workers' wages (3.8%) and overall inflation (3.5%). In fact, premiums have in-creased 87% over the past six years. Family health coverage now costs an average $11,480 annually, with workers paying an aver-age of $2,973 toward those premiums, about $1,354 more than in 2000. (2006 Employer Health Benefits Survey, 9/26/06)

- According to a federal analysis released in January 2007, in 2005, US health care spending increased 6.9% to almost $2.0 trillion, or $6,697 per person. The health care portion of gross domestic product (GDP) was 16.0%, slightly higher than the 15.9% share in 2004. This third consecutive year of slower health spending growth was largely driven by lower prescription drug expendi-tures, but spending for hospital, physician, and clinical services grew at similar rates to 2004. (Health Affairs, 1/9/07)

THE PROBLEM IS NOT GOING AWAY

The trends projected in 2003 did not hold up with the strong predic-tions, but the problem is not going away. It continues to worsen! The most recent statistics indicate that, although the problem has eased somewhat, the trend is still for health premiums to exceed the rate of growth of wages and inflation. This author was unable to find any evi-dence the federal government is even looking at the problem, let alone taking any action to bring this national tragedy under any control. After what we have seen with the banking and mortgage catastrophe that has engulfed the nation in a major recession, it is not a pleasant thought to predict what is going to happen to health care, even if the National Physicians Survey turns out to be incorrect in its predictions. With the bonuses being claimed by CEO's of health care plans at times approaching two billion dollars, the coming health care crash will make the banking industry debacle look like child's play.

The Henry J. Kaiser Family Foundation and the Health Research and Educational Trust acting in partnership remain the most important protectors of the public trust. The latest report available was the 2007 Kaiser/HRET Employer Health Benefits Survey. The 2008 statistics came out in late September 2008. The following facts from that report indicate that the dangerous trends are continuing.

- Health insurance premiums rose 6.1% in 2007, less rapidly than in recent years but still faster than wages and inflation.
- Annual premiums for family coverage now average $12,106, with workers paying $3,281.
- Since 2001, premiums for family coverage have increased 78%, while wages have gone up 19% and inflation 17%.
- Since 2000, the amount of businesses that offered employer-sponsored plans has dropped from 69 to 60%.
- Large corporations nearly all continue to offer some kind of health care product, but the number in smaller companies have fallen to 45%.

The onslaught on families and businesses continues. While the predictions made by the insurance industry have not held up, they were not far off. Kaiser President and CEO Drew E. Altman, Ph.D., said, "Every year health insurance becomes less affordable for families and businesses. Over the past six years, the amount families pay out of pocket for their share of premiums has increased by about $1,500." The disturbing problem is how the government remains so out of touch with the problems of their electorate.

IS HOPE FOR HEALTH CARE AUDACIOUS?

With the above taken into account, one must have been very worried about health care as the two presidential candidates campaigned to be elected. While they promoted their concern for the public, their "plans" demonstrated the hope that the public displays has truly become audacious. This health care professional is convinced that all politicians are out of touch with the true state of health care in America.

As well as our economy has held up over the years, our country simply cannot continue to pay the outrageous premiums the insurance industry is demanding. To provide for the kind of health care that Americans want and the kind of health care they are going to demand, a massive overhaul of the system has to occur; hopefully, before it all comes crashing down like the banking and mortgage industry has.

GAMES HEALTH INSURANCE COMPANIES PLAY

Insurance companies have developed exquisite business plans that all seem to be the same. These business plans are cleverly concocted stunts to deny health care providers proper payment. For example, simply delaying all doctors' pay by one day will earn an insurance company an average of $87,000. If they can delay the payment fifteen days, they will average $1.3 million in "savings" (i.e., ill-gotten profit). Fortunately, most states have prompt payment laws that require payment within thirty days. The tactics that these companies employ are, at the very least unethical, if not downright illegal.

Insurance companies have made it a science to skirt the rules. Their simplest ploy is just to deny the payment. The doctor's billing person-nel are tricked into believing they need to call the company, whereupon they are put on hold and directed through a maze of computerized phone menus. Once the telephone connection is finally made, the doc-tor's office is told that the insurance company "never received the bill." They trick the doctor's office into submitting the bill a second time, and the thirty-day period starts all over again.

If the doctor will not cooperate with their payment plans, instead of sending the doctor the check for the payment, they send it to the patient, who is likely to put a down payment on a new Toyota instead of paying his doctor's bill. The courts refuse to pursue them for fraud because the insurance company sent the money to the patient without instructions that it was to be used to pay their medical bills.

This was one major tool insurance companies used to take control of the billing process from the doctors. They set up a triangle whereby the patient/employer pays for the premiums. The patient seeks treatment from the doctor. The doctor cannot send the bill to the patient; he must bill the insurance company, and they pay whatever they want to.

In any other form of business, whoever seeks the service would pay for it. It would be much better for the doctors if they could just bill the patient directly for the service, but there are always a few unsavory doctors who approach insurance companies and say they will take less if they get all the patients.

If doctors got together to work out a collective bargaining plan, they would be hit with anti-trust suits. The government will always perse-cute and prosecute doctors who work together in any way. Three years ago in my local area, for example, it was reported by a doctor that there was a meeting attended by 100% of the OB-GYNs in the area. They agreed to set a limit for fees below which no one would ever go. No price fixing or individual fees discussed, only a watermark. This would insure them at least a working wage for their efforts. At the end of the meeting, they all shook hands and went home. However, one of the attendees then called all the insurance companies, told them what the doctors were up to, and said he would continue to take the low wages if he got all the patients.

Doctors are terrified of an empty waiting room, so everyone is paid the least amount possible, all because of one unsavory character. That is termed "competition," but competition should be based on a reasonable rate of pay, not some doctor who says he will take all the patients for a fee that cannot sustain a normal medical practice. That one doctor cannot possibly do all the work, so everyone takes the financial hit and insurance companies make millions. That is why the insurance companies send the check to the patient — to force the doctors to take the lower payment that will be mailed right to their office. In any other business, the government and the courts would hammer the opposition, but if it is a doctor, they just look the other way.

Another tactic is to ignore payment modifiers that would increase the doctor's reimbursements.

The above list could go on indefinitely. The insurance companies have become too powerful and are not given the strict treatment by the courts that any other business would be if they cheated their subscribers out of their payment. Fines of even $12 million, such as the one recently assessed against a large insurance company, are like pocket change to them. Delaying payments and getting a fine for that action only means they have to delay enough doctors' payments to pay the meager fine, if and when they get caught. The following day, they just resume what they were doing, knowing the fines are a drop in the bucket compared with what they make through these crude and unethical business practices.

The Result: A Broken Health Care System

What has resulted for the American citizen is a system of insurance that seeks to provide as little health care as possible for as high a premium as they can squeeze out of the public. Over the course of the war, the policies allowed by our government have resulted in the most expensive health care in the world with the least service to the patient.

The health care premium has become one of the primary instruments of destruction to our economy. Whether it is private insurance or workman's compensation, health care premiums are bleeding this economy dry.

An utterly inhumane insult occurred when Walt Tomala and his wife, Kathy had a meeting with a representative from their insurance company. Walt was forty years old when I met him. He had suffered from juvenile diabetes since he was a child, resulting in two kidney transplants. The meeting occurred when the Cleveland Clinic notified him that they had found a tissue match for a pancreas transplant that would solve his diabetes problems forever. His diabetes would have been controlled; his kidney would stop suffering the insults from diabetes, and his vascular system would get a well-needed rest from the problems of atherosclerosis (hardening of the arteries), a direct result of diabetes.

A representative of his insurance company told this man and his wife (she kept good notes) that "insurance and health care are no longer service industries in this country; they are hardcore businesses with a robust attention to the bottom line. Patients are no longer regarded as anything but financial liabilities and it is our job to eliminate our financial liabilities in favor of a profit and to pay our investors what they are due. We know that your disease is progressive and the statistics tell us that you have a very good chance of dying within the next five years, so we are prepared to provide you with all the needles and insulin you will need until you succumb to your illness. The fact that a procedure exists that could possibly prevent your demise is not in our financial interest and we will not cover that procedure."

The point here is that if someone is going to do business in health care, then it should be all-inclusive health care, not whatever makes the company the most money.

As a follow-up for the reader, in December 2008, I had the experience of being consulted on this same unfortunate patient. He had suffered a devastating CVA (stroke) following coronary artery bypass surgery, he was hemi-paretic (paralyzed on one side), and could no longer speak. There was nothing wrong with his mind. He was trapped inside a body that could not work, but he was conscious of everything around him. He could communicate basically, but it was tedious and difficult. Three months later, he suffered sixteen strokes in one night and lasted only a few more days. He lasted four years longer than the insurance company representative predicted, but true to their word, they provided him all the needles and insulin he required until he died.

This human tragedy could have been prevented. I hope the CEO of that health insurance company enjoyed his bonus, because the predictions that this patient would die came true, and I lost a patient whom I am proud to say had become a friend. America lost a great countryman, and his family lost a husband and father. Anathema!

On December 26, 2007, another incentive for me to expose the real inside of health care in America happened when a report on all the news media mentioned a young girl in California named Nataline Sarkysian. She was seventeen years old and dying of liver disease. She was very ill and was put at the top of the list for liver transplantation. Another "Managed Denial Company" refused to authorize the surgery. Local nurses organized a public protest and when the details of the situation reached the news media, the company began to worry about their public image, so they finally relented and allowed her the liver transplant. Sadly, the teenager died the next day before the surgery was completed.

This sort of story need never happen in America, but greed in the insurance industry has reached such heights that reports like these have become commonplace, as insurance has truly soured into a process that no longer places the highest value on patients' health or lives. They *have* become "hardcore" businesses that have a robust protection of the bottom line, no matter who or what tries to interfere in their profiteering. They have truly been transformed into modern-day selection agents with powers similar to the Nazi selection agents at death camps. They point to one line or another: "You live! You die!" "We do not cover that service." "We do not cover the payment of that drug." At the end of the process, some CEO takes a billion-dollar bonus, or like the Summa Health Plans here in Ohio, the insurance company pays millions to have a new football field named after them with dollars patients and employers have paid for their health care premiums. They scream that it is "advertising." I call it hubris.

Candidates for president of the US propose health care plans that purport to use the same insurance companies that have our citizens on the ropes, despite the fact that those same insurance companies have turned a system of total health care for a reasonable cost into a holocaust of denial of services, restrictions, record premiums, and unheard-of record profits. In response to the criticism, the insurance companies' spokesperson answered in a published remark in the summer of 2007 was "we know some adjustments need to be made, but we refuse to give up our profits." How fitting a response from an industry that is supposed to "insure" the health of the American people.

America has lost control of its health care system, and individuals have been taken advantage of through hubris, ego, self-indulgence, and greed. Insurance companies have become all too powerful. They are subject to only token oversight and are simply running wild in the marketplace, wielding way too much special interest power through massive donations to politicians for favors in legislation or simply inaction.

Something must be done.

Chapter Three

THE LIABILITY CRISIS

W HILE MEDICARE and insurance companies have taken their toll on the American health care system, the factor that has resulted in the highest amount of unnecessary health care cost is, without a doubt, the liability crisis.

THE DOCTOR'S BANE: MALPRACTICE LAWSUITS

In all human endeavors, people seem to find a way to bend the rules, distort the truth, and create new and ingenious methods to further their quest for money and power. The legal system is no different. Lawyers have been very diligent in their aim to redefine things for which a doctor can be brought to court.

The original intent of the law dealing with health care was to deal with "out of the standard of care" behavior. The courts originally stuck to that strict definition, but without written standards to guide the courts, and the overabundance of doctors willing to take a fee to testify against their colleagues, new and different definitions of what constitutes the "standard of care" have arisen.

The initial intent of the protective nature of a lawsuit was indeed honorable and necessary. There were a few bad doctors out there and there was some bad practice of medicine. Fortunately, the numbers were very small. Most doctors were good, but even good doctors are occasionally overwhelmed by the complexities of some medical care. Injuries to patients did occur but most of them did not necessarily result from bad treatment. Rather, they occurred from complications and unfortunate outcomes that no one had any real control over. Nevertheless, doctors created their own mess by not developing written standards of care, and lawyers just took advantage of the situation.

In addition, sentencing guidelines are present in all forms of criminal trials, but there are none in malpractice hearings. Some juries have awarded eight- and nine-figure amounts to people who have sued health care providers for malpractice. One award in Texas for $269 million stands out in my memory. The details of the case do not interest this author, but the audacity of a jury to award that much money to a patient is way out of bounds. Clearly, guidelines for measuring quality and worth or "value" of life are sorely needed. If we are going to control costs in medicine, we have to define guidelines for what each loss is worth, injury for injury, and stick to them.

THE RESULT: DEFENSIVE MEDICINE

What has resulted from doctors' fear of being sued for malpractice is a practice called "defensive medicine" that doctors utilize to try to head off a potential lawsuit. Since we will deal with this subject in detail later, suffice it to say here that these practices are expensive and represent the single largest expenditure in health care today.

Everyone suffers from this practice, but doctors have little protection left. Defensive medicine tactics take place in all aspects of medical practice. If we were to find a way to eliminate the practice of defensive medicine, the cost of medical care would drop precipitously. If any insurance plan seeks to cure the ills of health care in America, it *must* contain a solution to defensive medicine. Liability adds more unnecessary costs to the health care bill than anything else does, and that must change.

Sadly, the practice of defensive medicine is a problem generated by the obstinate refusal of doctors to give up the "art" of practicing medicine in favor of a more standardized and scientific approach to health care. Doctors could have written standards that did not abrogate their ability to tailor their treatments to different patients and still have at least some semblance of order in their profession. They should have defended those standards with their lives. Instead, the system degenerated into one that allowed doctors to use their "best" judgment in treating patients rather than stating specifically what constitutes the absolute agreed-upon and one-hundred-percent-practiced way to handle a problem.

Even lawyers have canons of ethics that guide their profession. Medicine is the only profession in which the standard of practice is referred to as the "generally agreed upon standard of care." By not coming up with precise standards of care, it was as if the doctors opted for the right to cannibalize their colleagues with whatever motivation there was to explain their willingness to testify in malpractice proceedings. The legal profession simply took what the doctors gave them. I cannot blame them.

Chapter Four

THE FALLOUT

IN ANY war, there are victims. Nurses, doctors, and allied health care personnel, the foot soldiers in health care, have borne the brunt of the attack on medicine. America is falling behind the rest of the world in quality of care because the system has placed burdens on the shoulders of, and roadblocks in the way of our nurses, doctors, and allied health associates. If America is ever to regain her place in the world with the best health care, the roadblocks have to be removed and the burdens lifted.

THE PLIGHT OF OUR NURSES

Nearly forty years ago, when America had the best health care in the world, doctors and nurses were able to work more harmoniously. The nurses were able to tend to their patients. Their written notes were enough for the doctor to interpret and do what needed to be done. There were fewer medical mistakes when things were much simpler. In 2004, Health Grades reported that the number of deaths from medical mistakes (195,000 a year) had nearly doubled from the number reported by an Institute of Medicine (IOM) report in 1999. This took place in just five short years, and Wikipedia reports that errors are becoming more common with increasing demands on a physician's attention.

Now, endless paperwork is the rule and the thought of "KISS" ("Keep It Simple, Stupid") has been replaced with a complicated and disorganized system of health care, with all the inherent problems we all hear about. As the chairman of my own hospital's Medical Record Committee, for example, I have witnessed firsthand the effects Medicare and the Joint Commission on the Accreditation of Hospitals rule changes have had on care in the hospital. The amount of paper-work a nurse has had to take on in daily duties has skyrocketed. With each new regulation come multifold increases in forms, flow sheets, and checklists.

ONE EXAMPLE

The scope of this discussion is a subject for an entire book, but just one example might help the reader understand the complexity of the problem.

Elderly people very often become confused in a hospital setting and climb out of bed, pull out catheters, pull out or disconnect IV lines, and the like. In doing so, they become at risk for injury. A few years ago, a new regulation was written on the monitoring of patients, who for their own protection need to be restrained, with either soft extremity restraints or a chest restraint, commonly called a "Posey restraint." The regulation stated that the nurse had to go check on the patient every fifteen minutes and several things needed to be documented each time the check was made.

Can you imagine how much of a burden this is on a nurse who is likely paired with another nurse on a floor with as many as fifty patients?

Why so often one might ask? It is probably because somewhere, some poor confused elderly person was injured by the restraints or possibly was able to get free of some of the restraints and was hanged.

One might then ask, why such a rigid program? Because families likely complained about "Mom" or "Dad" being "tied down."

In addition, since the nurse must spend monumentally more time charting and filling out the other endless list of required forms, flow sheets, and checklists, the presence of the nurse in the patient's room would necessarily be deficient. Therefore, this is one way to force the nurse into the room repeatedly, where in the past, each time the room was passed, a careful glance would have sufficed. Now the nurse has to document all the times the room was visited to check on the restraint and note them in the flow sheet. One liability suit would be enough to kick in the protective documentation.

FORMS, REGULATIONS, AND MORE FORMS

As the Medical Records Chairman, I have seen my share of forms not completely filled out because the nurse was too overburdened to do the task. In addition, I often wonder how many of the listings were backdated, as there really is no way to supervise this behavior.

For the record, this is just one regulation that implemented a specific behavior change. When America had the best medicine, our doctors were allowed to tend their patients instead of writing a book to fend off attorneys and Medicare audits. Death by medical mistake was nearly unheard of.

I am not sure the reader can really fathom the totality of the burdens placed upon our nurses and doctors in a system that was once called the best in the world due to the government interference in a system.

FEWER PERSONNEL

In addition, with Medicare and insurance cuts, America's hospitals have been forced to cut personnel. In doing so, a larger burden has been placed on our nurses, as fewer personnel means more documentation tasks belong to fewer people, resulting in furthering the distance between patients and nursing staff. With the lack of adequate staffing comes the inevitable mistakes from stressed out, over-tasked, over-burdened, tired, and increasingly unmotivated nurses becoming burned out and eventually exiting the profession.

The nursing profession was destroyed twenty years ago by the documentation requirements put in place in an attempt to avoid liability problems. Now the regulatory agencies are doing the same to doctors so that doctors are forced to spend more of their time tending to documentation rather than what they are trained in.

ALLIED HEALTH CARE

Allied health care, such as physical therapy, visiting nurses, makers of durable medical goods, and medical equipment companies, has become a huge industry. It is a necessary function in the care of patients, but some of the allied health professions have not been 100% honest in their dealings, either. Allied health has one of the highest fraud components in Medicare, and has resulted in the usual government knee-jerk reaction to assume everyone is dishonest. Oppressive rulemaking usually follows and the good services usually suffer in the face of more documentation that is rarely ever reviewed. In addition, one of the largest areas to be cut by government services and insurance companies is allied health services. As an example, in the very near future, Medicare is going to stop paying for physical therapy not conducted in the hospital.

I could go on and on about the victims in the war, but virtually everyone knows we have a nursing crisis on our hands. Doctors have been forced into retirement by liability insurance premiums, low reimbursements, and general poor morale. The nursing profession has suffered under the documentation madness, and allied health can barely offer services any more.

And things are getting worse

Despite modern technology, medicine is getting more difficult rather than simpler. Our health care providers are spending most of their time paying attention to things like documentation and record keeping, while day-to-day care suffers. In fact, this is the one of the largest areas of complaint by doctors. Our doctors are being made to become ward secretaries instead of utilizing their skills in the best possible manner.

Simply put, this has to stop. America is losing the War on Medical Care, and unless we release our best soldiers in the fight to preserve health in our country, we will lose. We need to allow doctors to devote their valuable time to paying attention to what is wrong with their patients, rather than spending their time worrying about how many items of a history and physical have to be recorded to head off a Medicare or insurance company audit. Instead of being glorified ward secretaries tending to endless flow charts no one ever pays attention, nurses need to return to being the eyes and ears of the doctors.

In addition, if doctors could write their own standards of care, care would become more uniform and regular, and they could use their talents to best serve their patients. Whatever maneuvering room they need to tailor their care to the individual patient can and should be entered into the equation, so doctors are not forced to feel they are practicing "cookbook" medicine. On the other hand, allowing the doctors to do as they please has not had a good track record over the years, as some physicians have used the system to seek additional income rather than concentrating on tending the sick. Appropriate controls should be the rule and can be done in a way to benefit the public and keep doctors' practices healthy. Standards of care algorithms can replace the need for endless documentation required for reimbursement and defensive medicine.

In summary, the control of medical practice has to be returned to the physicians. If America is ever to solve her medical woes, doctors and nurses need to be returned to their professional duties.

Chapter Five

OUR UN-AMERICAN HEALTH CARE SYSTEM

W ITH AMERICA being the richest country in the world, it seems improper that our health care system has degenerated into the state in which it presently rests. President Bush signed into law one of the most expensive bills ever to give many billions to a program to fight AIDS in Africa, while Americans suffer. Somewhere along the line, we have lost touch with our own health care system.

By chance, I came upon a very nice article that explains some of what my complaints are with health care in America.

On Sunday, April 6, 2008, an op-ed piece appeared in my local paper, *The Akron Beacon Journal*. It was authored by Steve Jacob, who is the publisher of the *Fort Worth Star-Telegram/Northeast* and is a Master's student in health policy and management at the University of North Texas Health Science Center in Fort Worth, Texas. I approached him and asked if I could reproduce his article in this book because I feel it strikes at the heart of the message I am trying to get across. He kindly gave his permission for the readers of this book to benefit from his writing and his experience.

The following is Steve Jacob's article in its entirety, as published by the *Akron Beacon Journal*.

OUR UN-AMERICAN HEALTH-CARE SYSTEM
BY STEVE JACOB

Fort Worth, Texas: It is hard to fathom how un-American the U.S. health-care system has become.

This has nothing to do with patriotism. It has everything to do with a system that forsakes ideals we hold dear: the sanctity of life, fairness, innovation and efficiency.

The Commonwealth Fund Commission on a High Performance Health System periodically does a U.S. health system scorecard comparing U.S. health outcomes to those of five other industrialized nations. It is brilliantly named, "Mirror, Mirror on the Wall," because our self-image is at odds with reality.

The United States was dead last in Commonwealth's last three comparisons. That, too, is un-American. This country is used to being the top dog in nearly every endeavor: finance, military might, diplomacy, athletics, and technology. President Bush has declared that he presides over a nation with "the best health-care system in the world."

To a limited degree, Bush is correct. The United States is the best nation on Earth to receive top-notch health care – if you are rich enough to afford it or fortunate enough to have private insurance.

But Bush's perspective appears to be a partisan approach. According to a recent Harris Interactive-Harvard poll, 68 percent of Republicans consider the U.S. health system the world's best, compared to 32 percent of Democrats and 40 percent of independents. Consider the following findings in published studies in the last 12 months that compare the United States to other industrialized nations. In America:

1. *You are more likely to die of a treatable condition.*

   In a Health Affairs article earlier this year, British researchers ranked leading industrialized nations on the rate of preventable deaths.

   The United States, which was 19th out of 19 nations, would have had 101,000 fewer preventable deaths annually if it had performed as well as the top three countries in the 2002-03 study. By gender, 23 percent of deaths in men and 32 percent of deaths in women were preventable with treatment. In another study, the U.S. life expectancy rank in 2004 was in 42nd place, down from 11th place two decades ago.

2. *You pay outrageous prices for shoddy service.*

   In 2005, the United States spent $6,697 per capita for health care – which is twice as much as five other industrialized nations. But its citizens were more likely to suffer from medical errors and be forced to go to the emergency room for care because of an inability to get a same-day appointment with a primary-care physician. Compared to five other nations with universal health care, the U.S. ranked fifth out of six on seeing a doctor promptly.

The argument that universal health care produces more inaccessible service is a myth.

3. *Our health care is primitive in its use of information technology.*
It's hard to believe that a nation that spawned Silicon Valley and Microsoft would be so far behind other countries on electronic medical records and medication prescriptions. Besides obvious inefficiencies, not employing technology makes it more difficult to coordinate care, measure outcomes, apply evidence-based clinical guidelines and investigate errors.

4. *Many people suffer because they cannot afford medical care.*
The United States is last in nearly every measure of equity because of the disparity in the quality of care received by those of means and those without. Americans are more likely than their counterparts to forgo treatment, skip recommended tests or leave prescriptions unfilled because of out-of-pocket costs. The common denominator in the consistently poor performance: The United States is the only industrialized nation without universal health care.

But there is much more to the story. Certainly, decreasing the number of uninsured would help these dismal numbers. But U.S. lifestyles and creature comforts also allow us to expend minimal energy. The resulting obesity and sedentary habits contribute mightily to our poor performance.

U.S. health care has become a caste system, stratified into the kind of social classes that the Founding Fathers so abhorred.

Those with private insurance rank on top for first-class service. In the middle are the underinsured, which have high deductibles in relation to their take-home pay. At the bottom are the uninsured. Even Medicare and Medicaid patients gradually are being squeezed out of the primary-care network because of inadequate provider reimbursement by the government.

And your class can literally be a life-or-death matter.

I am glad to see that Steve Jacob and I have both drawn similar conclusions to many of the issues. I am also proud and relieved to see that at least one other person has the courage to stand up and try to bring this issue to the attention of the American public.

A footnote to the above occurred with recent studies on the likelihood of dying with a preventable condition:

STUDY FINDS THAT MEDICAL ERRORS COST 238,337 LIVES, $8.8
BILLION OVER THREE YEARS.

HealthGrades, Inc. has released the results of its annual Patient Safety
in American Hospitals Study, which uses Medicare data to rank hospitals nationwide based on 16 patient safety indicators. The following are
among the findings of this year's study:

1. Of 270,491 deaths among patients who developed one or more
    patient safety incidents, 238,337 were potentially preventable.
2. The overall death rate among Medicare beneficiaries who devel-
    oped one or more patient safety incidents decreased almost 5
    percent from 2004 through 2006.
3. Four indicators of postoperative respiratory failure, postopera-
    tive pulmonary embolism or deep vein thrombosis, postoper-
    ative sepsis, and postoperative abdominal wound separation/
    splitting increased when compared to 2004.
4. Bed sores, failure to rescue, and post-operative respiratory failure
    accounted for 63.4 percent of all incidents. Overall, HealthGrades
    estimates that patient safety incidents cost Medicare $8.8 billion
    from 2004 through 2006.

It is difficult to disagree with any of the above. However, like many
Americans who are desperate, Mr. Jacob seems to feel that a government-controlled SPEC-type universal health care system is the answer
to the problems. That is where he and I might differ in how to correct
the problem.

I asked him if any of the above studies looked at the other industrial
nations and whether they are plagued with the liability crisis we have
in America. He replied he did not know of any. There is little or no liability problem in any other medical system in the world with the re-
sultant high costs and wasteful defensive medicine practices that occur
in American medical practices. Other countries simply do not investigate. Having interviewed doctors from Europe, I find that the government is not willing to interpose itself in the doctor-patient relationship
as is done here. For years, we heard that the fastest growing export of
American medicine was the malpractice suit, but it never caught on
anywhere else. In other societies, medical mistakes are not reported
as they are in our country. However, as soon as doctors are routinely
sued for their care, defensive medicine will take hold in those societies
also.

That is one glaring difference between our system and the rest of the world. The one statistic that states that Americans pay twice as much as the next nearest industrialized nation speaks to the fact that, just by lowering defensive and repetitive procedures in our country, our health care costs could go down by at least 50%, perhaps 60%!

The other glaring difference is the overbearing government interference in American health care with which other countries are not plagued. Their governments pay for health but without the government interference that we have.

This is a black eye on America. The world's richest country should not bear a "scarlet letter" because of a system that provides quality health care only for those who can afford it. America is better than that.

If it were not for the failings of the government to make its health care plan for the elderly work, it would be a logical step to ask the government to manage our problems as other countries have done. However, our citizens have indicated many times over that they do not want the rationing of health care that other countries have. Specifically, they repeatedly object to any notion of a SPEC program in America.

What the voters do not want is socialized medicine. SPEC-type medicine does not have a good record other than to say, "everyone is covered." If socialized medicine is so great, why do the Saudi royalty come to the US for their coronary artery bypasses? What we need is to reorganize the US health care system so it is available to everyone, not just Saudi kings.

I firmly believe America's time for universal care has come, but it would be a disaster to pawn this off on the federal government. The government cannot afford it and it cannot run it. A complete overhaul is necessary, but it should not be attempted before some commitments to the citizens of the US are made. These commitments should be in the form of resolutions we must accept — and can implement — as a society.

Chapter Six

REQUIREMENTS FOR A SUCCESSFUL UNIVERSAL HEALTH CARE PROGRAM

THIS (2008) presidential election cycle revealed how little our political leaders really know about health care. To them, "health care" means one thing and one thing only: votes. It is just another area for political positioning used to excite voters into thinking that they are somehow going to be covered miraculously with health care that someone else is going to pay for. In reality, based on their repeated behavior, career politicians do not care about health care for the masses. Health care to a career politician is nothing but a vehicle to be elected.

Unfortunately, the American voters have short memories. Every two, four or six years, the candidates resurrect their promises with fiery speeches and campaign rhetoric that is no more than political positioning, and the masses end up with nothing to show for their enthusiastic votes.

Health care is not a personal issue to the individual legislator because, as long as they keep being reelected, they have the best health care in the world. That health care plan is not available to the poor, the uneducated, the unemployed, the workers on the line at GM, or even bank presidents. They have set themselves up in a utopia the rest of us cannot even imagine. Despite the fact that they have been promising health care for decades, look at what we have. The same people who were uninsured in previous decades are still uninsured, and those who are "insured" are paying go-broke prices for minimal coverage that was heretofore-complete medical coverage.

Americans can see the problems. They frequently cry to their elected officials, but the open palms and smiles of the elected officials are but a guise. In the other hand, they hold the campaign donations given to them by insurance companies and lobbyists for medical supply companies, pharmaceutical companies, and promoters of medical gadgets.

How many decades have passed with those seeking elected positions shouting, "We're going to give you health care?" It never happens and this election cycle was no different. What the main players in the recent election were offering was simply not health care we are used to, need, or really deserve. It is *not* health care. It is a plea for the status quo on the Republican side and another try at government-controlled health care on the other, while still utilizing the same overcharging, undersupplying insurance companies for their solutions and maintaining the failing government entitlements. Voters beware!

WE MUST DO BETTER, AND WE MUST DO IT NOW

Changing the American health care system is a problem with far-reaching responsibility so a far-reaching solution is necessary. No medically ignorant politician is going to be our savior. Our salvation will not come out of any of the political "Health Care Plans" with which we were being besieged. Politicians simply know nothing about health care and they rely on consultants who would rather have a cushy government job than struggle in the trenches of medical practice.

Government types only know political or government solutions. It is quite evident that they cannot meet the needs of the American public; they can only satisfy the requirements of a government system.

The past four decades clearly indicate that the government simply needs to be eliminated as a choice for providing health care in the future. An appropriately designed program can be run in the private sector with appropriate controls, but regardless of the fact that 69% of Americans are interested in some type of universal health care, no one to date has come up with a reasonable plan — only more of the same political rhetoric and "programs."

FIRST, SOME RESOLUTIONS

No universal care plan can exist without a firm foundation to stand upon, and the plan I am going to outline in the latter half of this book is no exception. Therefore, I feel that first a few resolutions should be in order to return America to the highest ranking in medical care.

A FEW NECESSARY RESOLUTIONS

We must resolve that:

- We will not accept anything less than total complete health care.
- We will return to the days when we could go to any doctor or any hospital and have a complete major medical policy with full drug coverage.
- The system will be universal in nature: it will cover every US citizen, including the elderly. No one will be excluded.
- The plan will be affordable, even for those out of work.
- Everyone will have the same health care, from Congress on down. No one will get a better deal than anyone else does.
- The rationing of health care in other countries should not be an excuse for those people to come to the US to get care that is covered but unavailable in their own countries. This will be an American program, and there will be no foreigners coming to our country to obtain routine, non-emergency health care that their own countries could furnish but have chosen not to offer.
- America will continue to lead the world in medical innovation and treatments.
- We will eventually close the borders to foreign doctors and train our own young people to take care of our own.
- To accomplish that honorable goal, and to attract the best students to the profession and retain them, part of the package will be to insure that medical school is made affordable and that our doctors are well paid for their toils.
- The cost of medical school should somehow be subsidized by the public through taxes or loan forgiveness, as the cost of training a doctor is reaching nearly unattainable heights.
- The plan we enact will be self-governing through rigid practice controls designed by doctors and it will insure that individualization of patient care is not sacrificed and will not allow entrepreneurs to destroy the validity of our efforts.
- We will pay appropriately for our advances in drugs and technology, but not to the point that it breaks the back of the system.
- When we take the first step, we will never return to the disastrous ways of the past.
- We will forever keep politicians with their backbreaking government oversight programs and unnecessary regulations in Washington where they belong and out of the hospitals and doctors' offices where sick people are being cared for.
- We will return our nurses and doctors to their rightful duties

and free them from the burdens of the infernal documentation that robs sick people of their just attention.

- We will end the liability crisis that pervades our health care empire and agree to handle our problems in a different manner without taking away any of the protection the public currently enjoys.
- The present model of small group insurance plans must be replaced by one single universal program that allows the cost to be spread across our entire population.

Finally:

- We must simply resolve that we will succeed, no matter how long it takes or how difficult this task.

WE CAN DO IT

All this is possible in such a way that health care will be affordable, universal, and simply the best the world can realize, not because it is a dream, but because it is a real life attainable goal.

The public has to be made aware that they really control the purse strings and that when a viable alternative to the bullying by the government and insurance companies and hospital administrators is made available, they can choose to exercise their supreme power over all of them.

Americans repeatedly exclaim that they want their health care returned to the hands of their doctors. Universal health care need not be a frightful undertaking. American doctors can design their own health care system without overbearing governmental control. A privately run universal health care system is not out of the question. With appropriate controls and a sensible approach to things, we *can* do this.

Remember the proverb: "If one man dreams, it is only a dream, but if an entire nation dreams, it can be a reality."

Part Two:

THE SOLUTION TO THE PROBLEM

We shall now explore the depths of the plan. It is simple enough for the common man to read and understand so I feel comfortable laying it out. Minor details may need to be added, subtracted, or revised as it is put into existence, but the plan itself is sound. Throughout the explanation that is to come, I shall attempt to explain the points where the present plans, Medicare, and entitlements fail, and how this system will prevail. Keep in mind that everything you are about to read is a plan that is driven by rigid standards of care that will determine everything in the plan.

Chapter Seven

PROPOSED HEALTH CARE PLAN

T HIS CHAPTER will attempt to present the main points of the health care plan proposed by our recently elected President, Barack Obama. There are many points in his program, but like much of what we heard during the campaign, it describes the problems that he wants to solve without a solution. I think Mr. Obama hit on several important topics, but his plan is not nuts and bolts health care; it is idealism. Mr. Obama is really out of touch with what is needed now and in the future.

MASSACHUSETTS STEPPED UP FIRST

Massachusetts took the lead in attempting to gain control of its health care mess. Its program requires that everyone be insured. Essentially everyone has a "plan," but not everyone can afford complete coverage, so large holes in coverage exist. People may pick from all the various plans that are available, but none of the plans is complete as managed denial runs rampant.

A politician's answer is to have a "plan," but with deductibles that are more than some people can afford and with co-pays for everything, the lower income and the working poor still have next-to-no ability to enter the system except to take advantage of the safety net of emergency services when life-threatening conditions erupt. Still they count in the numbers as people who have "health care."

AND THE WINNERS ARE: THE INSURANCE COMPANIES!

Once again, the winners in this scenario are the insurance companies. They get to sell their insurance policies to everyone and keep huge profits in return for skeleton policies. The only exception that makes this plan stand out is that it brings everyone to the actuary table. If managed right, they would spread the costs across the entire population. Unfortunately, they fall short by allowing the bullying insurance companies to limit care and take huge profits in doing so.

In June of 2008, Massachusetts levied fines against 95,000 people in the state for not purchasing health care. No one really knows why they did not purchase the health care mandated by the state, but one can surely wager that the majority of them are working poor who just could not afford the premiums.

Is this a first in American history? The government is mandating that people purchase insurance for health care. When one looks at the record states have had requiring people to purchase insurance for their cars, it was an easy call to bet there would be those who would defy the law with health care as well. Levying a fine on someone for not purchasing health care does not make it any easier to pay the premium *and* the fine. That makes as much sense as charging $20 to someone's checkbook for bouncing a check when there is already no money in it.

Yahoo News reported in 2008 that Massachusetts suddenly had more people with insurance than ever before, even with the 95,000 people who did not purchase insurance as mandated by law. The problem came when the newly insured people found it next to impossible to find a doctor willing to take them on as patients. There were simply not enough doctors to absorb the load, and Massachusetts has the highest density of doctors per capita in the US. This illustrates one of the problems we face with any kind of universal health care; not enough doctors. Many have quit, retired early, or simply have been driven out of business. This is bad news with Medicare preparing to descend upon America's doctors with their RACs audits and the National Physicians' Foundation study declaring that half of America's doctors are fed up with practicing medicine and will leave the entire country lacking in available doctors. It is obvious that, to bring many of these doctors out of retirement and encourage them to resume their duties, we need some kind of plan that insures doctors have adequate pay and conditions to practice.

BARACK OBAMA ON HEALTH CARE

If you have not read the President's Health care plan, you should do so. It is reproduced here so the reader can realize that this plan is remarkable because it is wide ranging and covers lots of territory, but it is written as if someone is trying to impress us with individual health care issues that seem to elicit strong feelings. It is, however replete with idealism and government control; both rarely, if ever are successful. It is not a bad program, clearly the best of the three major candidates in the 2008 election. It is a prelude to arguments claiming that America needs a government-controlled health care plan. I think not, and the program you will discover in the following chapters can cover anything in the following health care plan sponsored by Barack Obama at a fraction of the cost. Government does best when it governs within the Constitution. Micromanagement of a doctor-patient relationship is not spelled out in the Constitution.

BARACK OBAMA'S PLAN

Millions of Americans are uninsured or underinsured because of rising medical costs: 47 million Americans — including nearly 9 million children — lack health insurance with no signs of this trend slowing down.

Health care costs are skyrocketing: Health insurance premiums have risen 4 times faster than wages over the past 6 years.

Too little is spent on prevention and public health: The nation faces epidemics of obesity and chronic diseases as well as new threats of pandemic flu and bioterrorism. Yet despite all of this less than 4 cents of every health care dollar is spent on prevention and public health.

Quality, Affordable and Portable Coverage for All

- **Obama's Plan to Cover Uninsured Americans:** Obama will make available a new national health plan to all Americans, including the self-employed and small businesses, to buy affordable health coverage that is similar to the plan available to members of Congress. The Obama plan will have the following features:

  1. Guaranteed eligibility. No American will be turned away from any insurance plan because of illness or pre-existing conditions.

  2. Comprehensive benefits. The benefit package will be similar to that offered through Federal Employees Health Benefits Program (FEHBP), the plan members of Congress have. The plan will cover all essential medical services, including pre-

ventive, maternity and mental health care.
3.   Affordable premiums, co-pays and deductibles.
4.   Subsidies. Individuals and families who do not qualify for Medicaid or SCHIP but still need financial assistance will receive an income-related federal subsidy to buy into the new public plan or purchase a private health care plan.
5.   Simplified paperwork and reined in health costs.
6.   Easy enrollment. The new public plan will be simple to enroll in and provide ready access to coverage.
7.   Portability and choice. Participants in the new public plan and the National Health Insurance Exchange (see below) will be able to move from job to job without changing or jeopardizing their health care coverage.
8.   Quality and efficiency. Participating insurance companies in the new public program will be required to report data to ensure that standards for quality, health information technology and administration are being met.
- **National Health Insurance Exchange:** The Obama plan will create a National Health Insurance Exchange to help individuals who wish to purchase a private insurance plan. The Exchange will act as a watchdog group and help reform the private insurance market by creating rules and standards for participating insurance plans to ensure fairness and to make individual coverage more affordable and accessible. Insurers would have to issue every applicant a policy, and charge fair and stable premiums that will not depend upon health status. The Exchange will require that all the plans offered are at least as generous as the new public plan and have the same standards for quality and efficiency. The Exchange would evaluate plans and make the differences among the plans, including cost of services, public.
- **Employer Contribution:** Employers that do not offer or make a meaningful contribution to the cost of quality health coverage for their employees will be required to contribute a percentage of payrolls toward the costs of the national plan. Small employers that meet certain revenue thresholds will be exempt.
- **Mandatory Coverage of Children:** Obama will require that all children have health care coverage. Obama will expand the number of options for young adults to get coverage; including allowing young people up to age 25 to continue coverage through their parents' plans.

- **Expansion Of Medicaid and SCHIP:** Obama will expand eligibility for the Medicaid and SCHIP programs and ensure that these programs continue to serve their critical safety net function.
- **Flexibility for State Plans:** Due to federal inaction, some states have taken the lead in health care reform. The Obama plan builds on these efforts and does not replace what states are doing. States can continue to experiment, provided they meet the minimum standards of the national plan.

LOWER COSTS BY MODERNIZING THE U.S. HEALTH CARE SYSTEM

- **Reducing Costs of Catastrophic Illnesses for Employers and Their Employees:** Catastrophic health expenditures account for a high percentage of medical expenses for private insurers. The Obama plan would reimburse employer health plans for a portion of the catastrophic costs they incur above a threshold if they guarantee such savings are used to reduce the cost of workers' premiums.
- **Helping Patients:**
  1. Support disease management programs. Seventy five percent of total health care dollars are spent on patients with one or more chronic conditions, such as diabetes, heart disease and high blood pressure. Obama will require that providers that participate in the new public plan, Medicare or the Federal Employee Health Benefits Program (FEHBP) utilize proven disease management programs. This will improve quality of care, give doctors better information and lower costs.
  2. Coordinate and integrate care. Over 133 million Americans have at least one chronic disease and these chronic conditions cost a staggering $1.7 trillion yearly. Obama will support implementation of programs and encourage team care that will improve coordination and integration of care of those with chronic conditions.
  3. Require full transparency about quality and costs. Obama will require hospitals and providers to collect and publicly report measures of health care costs and quality, including data on preventable medical errors, nurse staffing ratios, hospital-acquired infections, and disparities in care. Health plans will also be required to disclose the percentage of premiums that go to patient care as opposed to administrative costs.

- **Ensuring Providers Deliver Quality Care:**
  1. Promote patient safety. Obama will require providers to report preventable medical errors and support hospital and physician practice improvement to prevent future occurrences.
  2. Align incentives for excellence. Both public and private insurers tend to pay providers based on the volume of services provided, rather than the quality or effectiveness of care. Providers who see patients enrolled in the new public plan, the National Health Insurance Exchange, Medicare and FEHBP will be rewarded for achieving performance thresholds on outcome measures.
  3. Comparative effectiveness research. Obama will establish an independent institute to guide reviews and research on comparative effectiveness, so that Americans and their doctors will have the accurate and objective information they need to make the best decisions for their health and well-being.
  4. Tackle disparities in health care. Obama will tackle the root causes of health disparities by addressing differences in access to health coverage and promoting prevention and public health, both of which play a major role in addressing disparities. He will also challenge the medical system to eliminate inequities in health care through quality measurement and reporting, implementation of effective interventions such as patient navigation programs, and diversification of the health workforce.
  5. Insurance reform. Obama will strengthen antitrust laws to prevent insurers from overcharging physicians for their malpractice insurance and will promote new models for addressing errors that improve patient safety, strengthen the doctor-patient relationship and reduce the need for malpractice suits.
- **Lowering Costs Through Investment in Electronic Health Information Technology Systems:** Most medical records are still stored on paper, which makes it hard to coordinate care, measure quality or reduce medical errors and which costs twice as much as electronic claims. Obama will invest $10 billion a year over the next five years to move the U.S. health care system to broad adoption of standards-based electronic health information systems, including electronic health records, and will phase in requirements for full implementation of health IT. Obama will

ensure that patients' privacy is protected.

- **Lowering Costs by Increasing Competition in the Insurance and Drug Markets:** The insurance business today is dominated by a small group of large companies that has been gobbling up their rivals. There have been over 400 health care mergers in the last 10 years, and just two companies dominate a full third of the national market. These changes were supposed to make the industry more efficient, but instead premiums have skyrocketed by over 87 percent.

    1. Barack Obama will prevent companies from abusing their monopoly power through unjustified price increases. His plan will force insurers to pay out a reasonable share of their premiums for patient care instead of keeping exorbitant amounts for profits and administration. His new National Health Exchange will help increase competition by insurers.

    2. Lower prescription drug costs. The second-fastest growing type of health expenses is prescription drugs. Pharmaceutical companies are selling the exact same drugs in Europe and Canada but charging Americans more than double the price. Obama will allow Americans to buy their medicines from other developed countries if the drugs are safe and prices are lower outside the U.S. Obama will also repeal the ban that prevents the government from negotiating with drug companies, which could result in savings as high as $30 billion. Finally, Obama will work to increase the use of generic drugs in Medicare, Medicaid, and FEHBP and prohibit big name drug companies from keeping generics out of markets.

FIGHT FOR NEW INITIATIVES

- **Advance the Biomedical Research Field:** As a result of biomedical research the prevention, early detection and treatment of diseases such as cancer and heart disease is better today than any other time in history. Barack Obama has consistently supported funding for the national institutes of health and the national science foundation. Obama strongly supports investments in biomedical research, as well as medical education and training in health-related fields, because it provides the foundation for new therapies and diagnostics. Obama has been a champion of research in cancer, mental health, health disparities, global health, women and children's health, and veterans' health. As president, Obama will strengthen funding for biomedical research, and better improve the efficiency of that research by improving coordination both within government and across government/private/non-profit partnerships. An Obama administration will ensure that we translate scientific progress into improved approaches to disease prevention, early detection and therapy that is available for all Americans.

- **Fight AIDS Worldwide.** There are 40 million people across the planet infected with HIV/AIDS. As president, Obama will continue to be a global leader in the fight against AIDS. Obama believes in working across party lines to combat this epidemic and recently joined Senator Sam Brownback (R-KS) at a large California evangelical church to promote greater investment in the global AIDS battle.

- **Support Americans with Disabilities:** As a former civil rights lawyer, Barack Obama knows firsthand the importance of strong protections for minority communities in our society. Obama is committed to strengthening and better enforcing the Americans with Disabilities Act (ADA) so that future generations of Americans with disabilities have equal rights and opportunities. Obama believes we must restore the original legislative intent of the ADA in the wake of court decisions that have restricted the interpretation of this landmark legislation. Barack Obama is also committed to ensuring that disabled Americans receive Medicaid and Medicare benefits in a low-cost, effective and timely manner. Recognizing that many individuals with disabilities rely on Medicare, Obama worked with Senator Ken Salazar (D-CO) to urge the department of health and human services to provide clear and reliable information on the Medicare prescription drug benefit and to ensure that the Medicare recipients were protected from fraudulent claims by marketers and drug plan agents.

- **Improve Mental Health Care.** Mental illness affects approximately one in five American families. The National Alliance on Mental Illness estimates that untreated mental illnesses cost the U.S. more than $100 billion per year. As President, Obama will support mental health parity so that coverage for serious mental illnesses are provided on the same terms and conditions as other illnesses and diseases.

- **Protect Our Children from Lead Poisoning.** More than 430,000

American children have dangerously high levels of lead in their blood. Lead can cause irreversible brain damage, learning disabilities, behavioral problems, and, at very high levels, seizures, coma and death. As president, Obama will protect children from lead poisoning by requiring that child care facilities be lead-safe within five years.

- **Reduce Risks of Mercury Pollution.** More than five million women of childbearing age have high levels of toxic mercury in their blood, and approximately 630,000 newborns are born at risk every year. Barack Obama has a plan to significantly reduce the amount of mercury that is deposited in oceans, lakes, and rivers, which in turn would reduce the amount of mercury in fish.

- **Support Americans with Autism.** More than one million Americans have autism, a complex neurobiological condition that has a range of impacts on thinking, feeling, language, and the ability to relate to others. As diagnostic criteria broaden and awareness increases, more cases of autism have been recognized across the country. Barack Obama believes that we can do more to help autistic Americans and their families understand and live with autism. He has been a strong supporter of more than $1 billion in federal funding for autism research on the root causes and treatments, and he believes that we should increase funding for the Individuals with Disabilities Education Act to truly ensure that no child is left behind. More than anything, autism remains a profound mystery with a broad spectrum of effects on autistic individuals, their families, loved ones, the community, and education and health care systems. Obama believes that the government and our communities should work together to provide a helping hand to autistic individuals and their families

A DOCTOR'S CONCLUSION

President Obama campaigned on this plan to seek to insure all Americans. This is a great goal, but the new President has his hands full with a nearly destroyed economy with businesses failing right and left, banks and mortgage companies failing, people losing jobs, and health care premiums skyrocketing. His plan to raise taxes to pay for his plan should be put on hold because raising taxes in the midst of a huge recession could throw the country into depression, as it once did in 1929.

The shortcomings of President Obama's program are many. The most important one is that he makes no effort to bring the health insurance industry or the Medicare disaster under control. He gives lip service to trial lawyers, as he flirts with the already failed tort reform system as the answer to liability problems. Medicare is collapsing under its own weight, and insurance companies are simply ripping off the public. What good does it do to have a universal health care system without radically controlling the insurance companies that are the crux of the present problem?

At this writing, he has been in office for eleven weeks. His recently completed State of the Union message indicated that he intends to spend unprecedented amounts of money. Reports are that he has signed into law a bill that spends in excess of $600 billion of borrowed taxpayers' money. Already he claims that his health care policy will be paid for by taxing the rich, cutting reimbursements to hospitals, clinics and doctors; none of which can afford any more cuts.

The health care plan you are going to learn about will give Mr. Obama the chance to reach all of his goals in health care without raising one dime of taxes other than to pursue premiums for those on entitlement programs. In addition, it will unburden him of the Medicare and Medicaid collapse about to happen. It will also give him the opportunity to prevent a major catastrophe in the medical profession that is about to occur if the recent National Physician's Foundation Survey is to be believed.

President Obama must be careful not to fall into the trap of believing that "universal" SPEC type health care for the American public does not mean rationing. The envelope that has "health care" written on the outside had better be full.

Chapter Eight

STEP I IN RECONSTRUCTING HEALTH CARE IN AMERICA

THE FIRST step in changing anything is always the most difficult because one must overcome inertia to get moving, and there is a huge amount of inertia to overcome here. If all were well in America, we would not have a problem. There are complaints being registered, but the public is waiting for someone to solve the problem for them.

WHAT DOES IT REALLY TAKE TO MAKE THE PUBLIC YELL 'UNCLE'?

Like all aspects of American life, the population needs the desire to change before any meaningful change can occur. However, the health care environment is so rotten right now, that there could be no better time to introduce this plan and overcome the inertia and resistance to movement that is inherently in the way. It is time for Americans to take control of their health care system.

STEP I: A COMMON MEDICAL RECORD

Step I initiates the program by eliminating one huge obstacle in health care today. In the film, *Cool Hand Luke*, there is a very famous line still conjured up even today: "What we have here is a failure to communicate!" Without a doubt, the largest single problem we have in our health care system is *a failure to communicate*. If we are ever going to revolutionize medicine in America, health care practitioners need to be able to communicate easily with each other. Right now, except for the next-to-useless telephone, fax and mail, no communication avenue exists that allows the type of communication we need.

I have been on the Medical Records Committee at my local hospital for twenty-five years, and I have been the Chairman for nearly two decades. I have observed a glaring deficit in the abilities of all parties to communicate. The bottom line here is that there is not a single medical record form that is common to each medical office, hospital, or otherwise.

Presently, a patient's medical record is a hodgepodge of hand-scribbled illegible notes, dictated records, and computerized medical records. Transferring these records to any other health care facility is a nightmare because none of the records is in a common form. Today, except in rare instances, all records are duplicated on a copy machine, and transferred via courier, fax, or mail. Therefore, every time this happens, we end up with two huge piles of paper requiring storage. The amount of money wasted is monumental. The military has proven over and over again that the best way to make things work properly is to make things uniform. *Creating a uniform medical record is a must to facilitate the introduction of a Universal Health Care Plan.*

Several years ago, Medicare/Medicaid required all doctors to go to an electronic billing system and then on to an electronic medical record (EMR). In typical American way, thousands of companies saw the dollar signs and produced their own version of a utopian EMR. These computer programs are expensive, averaging over $30,000 each for a solo practice. (One of the local heart groups near me indicated that the software they use in their office cost over $250,000) Unless the doctor belongs to a big group that can share the record and spread the cost, it is almost prohibitive to use a computer program, never mind the fact that once the program is purchased, it is already obsolete. In addition, it requires a computer guru to maintain it.

It is a burden to have a program that must be updated yearly, as Medicare/Medicaid finds new ways to choke the doctors financially with their ICD-9 codes, CPT codes, and their confusing modifiers and CCI edits. Someone has to update that program continually, and it costs money to do it — lots of it.

Many doctors have confided to me that they simply retired or went out of business because they could not pay for the EMR. What the doctors failed to realize is that Medicare/Medicaid mandated the EMR for one reason and one reason only. They did not care if the records communicated with each other. They only wanted an EMR so they did not have to try to decipher poor handwriting. This made the job of auditing doctors infinitely easier for them, but it hogtied everyone else. One huge government bureaucracy usurped the power and instituted change without taking into consideration the important needs of all the others that must access the information in the medical record. So instead of one distinct record that all can access, we have now wasted millions of dollars on thousands upon thousands of different computer programs that cannot interchange information.

In my own situation, I work with three major hospitals and two surgery centers. The EMR at one hospital does not communicate with the EMR at another, and none of the three EMRs can "talk" to my office software, nor can other doctors' offices communicate with my software. Furthermore, simply going from hospital to hospital puts a practitioner in a maze of frustration, as one tries to remember which form is used to order a blood chemistry profile or even what the test is called at each place. In addition, when there is an attempt to try to communicate records, the requesting hospital rarely knows what to ask for, so they just ask for it all. This raises the cost and complicates the fact that the medical record is doubled every time it is copied, not to mention the privacy issues, as these records are transported between locations.

Recently, I was asked to do a disability evaluation for the US Labor Department. A box of records was delivered to my office that contained over two thousand pages. It took me nearly eighteen months to complete the job and provide the government with the consultation they sought. There were so many repetitions that I finally separated the individual forms into separate piles. In reality, the record had been duplicated so many times that I had about thirty different piles of the same page and one page was duplicated fifty-four times. Do we really want the federal government to direct this problem?

LET US ALL GET ON THE SAME PAGE

The premise I am promoting here, as the first step is a generalized reorganization of the entire country to put everyone "on the same page," — literally. Communication between health care entities would be facilitated if the medical record on both ends looked the same, used the same terminology, the same software, had the same forms, and even the same print font. In a Universal Health Care Plan, *everything* must be universal. This means that a patient who walks into a medical office in Phoenix, Arizona has the same History and Physical form, the same laboratory requisition, and the same operative report or Emergency Room documents as a patient in San Francisco, the Mayo Clinic, or

Betsy Johnson Hospital in Dunn, North Carolina. That way, if the patient has to seek care at another institution, the medical record can be sent electronically to the practitioner who needs the information.

Instituting a common medical record would also go a long way toward *standardizing health care practices*, another must in a Universal Health Care Plan. It would provide an easier way of tracking, reviewing and, if necessary, policing health care providers. If someone walks into a clinic on Tybee Island, South Carolina, he/she will be evaluated and treated in exactly the same way that he/she would be in Cedars Sinai Hospital in California. Human beings in South Carolina have the same human make up as those in California, so why should they have to deal with different approaches to their health care? In medicine, there is only one right way to do things. A common medical record will help make that possible.

Mr. Obama has recognized that the medical record needs to be shifted to an electronic record. His answer is to raise $10 billion in taxes every year for five years to make this happen. I can see another huge bureaucracy starting. As we will see, this habit of throwing money at a problem turns out, in the end, to be in itself a problem. It is so unnecessary.

A COMMON MEDICAL RECORD WILL REDUCE COST

Three problems in medicine today costs the public an estimated 60% of the health care bill. A common medical record is necessary if we are to eliminate these three issues that plague this country and raise the cost of health care astronomically.

1) DEFENSIVE MEDICINE

Defensive medicine is the practice doctors have developed whereby any and all diagnostic tests are ordered in an attempt to document the chart so that it cannot be used against them in a lawsuit. It also consists of doctors ordering tests to make sure a condition that could harm the patient could not possibly be missed.

For example, every year, about eight million people are treated for dizziness, which can be caused by a malignant brain tumor. The chance of being diagnosed with a primary malignant brain tumor, however, is only 0.67% for males and 0.51% for females — about 1%. However, since a brain tumor is one of the most serious problems faced by patients, it would behoove the doctor not to miss it, thinking the dizziness could be caused by common things, such as an ear infection, viral infection, and allergies. Because the repercussions of missing a brain tumor are so disastrous for doctors (such as a malpractice suit, having his insurance rates raised, or even being dropped from his policy), they are likely to choose an MRI for *every patient* who presents with dizziness.

If a doctor did not obtain an MRI, as with all cancers, the patient would eventually show up with advanced symptoms in the future, and it would likely come out that the patient had seen his doctor with the symptom of dizziness at some time in the past, when there could have been a better chance of curing the disease. Because that one penalty is so severe, many doctors order *an MRI on every person* seen with dizziness to protect against the inevitable lawsuit. In the present liability market, one suit could very well cost a very good doctor his career. So, the answer is to order 7,994,104 unnecessary MRI exams. Each MRI costs $1600. If we divide the number of MRIs that are potentially ordered in this defensive tactic by the number of brain tumors that are actually found each year, it works out to a cost of *over $250,000 for each primary malignant brain tumor found.*

If only one MRI were ordered for each brain tumor, the cost would only be $1500 for each tumor that is diagnosed every year. The reader has to realize that to treat just this one diagnosis is *167 times more expensive* than it needs to be.

Now let us factor in the emotion that occurs with just this one diagnosis. Very few people survive malignant brain tumors. Once diagnosed, these patients and their families are angry. The emotional costs to the doctor are equally as costly. No doctor wants to be faced with telling someone they have a brain tumor and they are going to die, but the doctor does not want to be saddled with the blame for this tragic event either, so defensive medicine rules.

We are paying too much for our medical care in this country, as this example shows. This one factor is why other countries have relatively inexpensive health care compared to ours. This is one more expensive issue of defensive medicine that could be effectively eliminated by a written standard that lays out a plan for when and if an MRI is necessary. If the reader will only realize that doctors face this same dilemma for every encounter and every diagnosis with a patient, it becomes easy to understand why medicine is so expensive in America.

Health insurance companies say paying for defensive medicine represents 25% of their costs, but I can say from experience that it actually represents 50% or more. Doctors have a common thought that goes through their mind when they practice a defensive style of medicine, simply, "If you think of it, do it." This raises the cost of health care without providing service for the expenditure. A common medical record will facilitate the practice of standardizing medical care, which in turn, will help keep doctors in line with the recommended diagnostic and treatment protocols. It will make it easier to follow the course of treatment, review results, make changes if necessary, and protect the doctors against frivolous suits if the record shows the doctor has remained within the standardized care plan.

2) REPETITIVE MEDICINE

The second problem involves what is called "repetitive medicine." Repetitive medicine occurs when doctors are forced to repeat evaluation and management tasks, such as history and physical examinations, laboratory work, and imaging, as patients are forced to see new doctors as their insurance keeps changing. If the doctor being left behind is not on the new plan, then the new doctor is required to do a new history and physical examination. The laboratory work and images are likely to be repeated, especially if a new hospital is involved. It is a huge expense.

Repetitive medicine occurs because of a lack of a common medical record. It occurs because everyone is trying to get bottom dollar for high-priced health care. Employers constantly seek other health care plans when their small group rates go up astronomically. Patients are forced to leave their traditional hospitals and doctors by negotiating a better price for the insurance company.

3) ENTREPRENEURIAL MEDICINE

The third problem is what I call entrepreneurial medicine. This occurs as doctors slip outside the bounds of ethics and do something for money rather than as part of a proper health care ritual. Perhaps a doctor has purchased an MRI and refers many patients for an expensive test that would not ordinarily be necessary. It also occurs as some doctors participate in a cottage industry providing expert testimony against a colleague in malpractice litigation.

AN EXAMPLE

Let us follow a patient with moderate health care issues, as he is goes through the system. Let us say he is fifty-five years old, Caucasian, has had a couple of cardiac events, diabetes, smokes, and has mild asthma. He is also overweight, with degenerative arthritis in his back, hips, and knees. In addition, he has hypertension. His employer is on the verge of going out of business because his health care premiums are killing him, so he drops Insurance Company "A" to accept a cheaper policy from Insurance Company "B". It does not offer as much service, but it is called "health insurance" just the same.

Our patient has always gone to Doctor A and Hospital A. He has been very satisfied with the relationship with Doctor A. As he now has insurance with Company B, he has a choice of still staying with Doctor A and Hospital A, but he must either pay some percentage of his medical bills to stay with him because they are "out of network," or accept the fact that he has to find a new doctor. He chooses Doctor B and Hospital B because he cannot afford to pay the additional costs.

Doctor B now must take an initial E & M (Evaluation and Management) history and do a complete physical, from which he finds out that Patient A has all the above health care problems. Next, now that he has assumed the care of this patient, he is faced with the requirement to become thoroughly familiar with the health care problems, and that usually requires a workup for each of the problems.

Enter defensive medicine and entrepreneurial medicine. The doctor is aware of the problem of each patient being a potential plaintiff, so he orders all the tests he feels he needs to document his chart and potentially head off a lawsuit if something goes wrong. In addition, he might benefit if he takes X-rays, draws the blood, or looks at the urine in his own office, so those are done, adding to the bill. If any consultations with specialists are required, they are done, and the same process with defensive — and sometimes entrepreneurial — medicine occurs all over again. This is all standard practice in America.

One might ask what happened to his medical records. From personal experience, I have found that trying to collect a complete record on a patient is nearly impossible. Frequently, the records that one acquires are incomplete. Hospitals are not cooperative in transferring records to a competing hospital, plus the doctor is extremely lucky if he gets the records in a timely fashion. If the doctor creates his own medical records with handwritten notes, that only complicates things, because many doctors' handwriting is illegible. Misinterpretation of an illegible note could cause another doctor to initiate the wrong treatment and lead to an injury, death, and most certainly a lawsuit, so repetition or redundancy results.

Let us assume that after a year all is well. If the insurance company is in a regional or local group, the cost of supporting all the subscribers determines the premiums. If the group had a bad year, meaning there were lots of costs generated by things, such as heart attacks, cancer, or total joint replacement, the company could go below the bottom line into the red. That will require a raise in premiums or the company could go out of business. All the employers on that plan will be faced with a rise in health care costs.

Some employers will not be able to tolerate the increase and will try to shift to another company. In that case, our hypothetical patient above could be forced once again to switch doctors and hospitals, and the new E & M history and physical, the tests, and consultations would all be repeated.

The reader might be wondering why the new doctor does not just get the other doctor's records. That is a good question. In today's liability market, many doctors are not eager to send their records to another doctor because the new doctor might be critical of his care, causing a malpractice suit. Likewise, the new doctor is usually unwilling to trust the previous doctor's practice habits, knowledge, and experience. If the previous doctor has made an error, the new doctor could be at risk of a lawsuit if he does not explore the problem himself. Furthermore, if the records are incomplete or illegible, the new doctor is taking a chance by not having all the records at hand. All this goes to say that retrieving the records, copying the records, and paying for the records to be copied and forwarded heavily penalize the system with repeated costs and time spent in doing so. There is a heavy cost to duplicating the record again and again.

Insurance companies and employers force the trade of patients between doctors and hospitals back and forth like this all the time.

How a common digital medical record will change things

Let us look at how a common digital medical record will change things without even considering controls on insurance company profits.

In our ideal scenario, every doctor and hospital is now on a common digital medical record that can be accessed by a computer program. As in the example above, Doctor A has been taking care of Patient A when Patient A is forced to go to Hospital B and Doctor B. Patient A's medical record — including all his X-rays, cardiac tests, and his laboratory work — has been kept in a data bank. Once Patient A visits Doctor B, the appropriate security codes are exchanged and Doctor B can see all of the records from Doctor A and Hospital A. He does not require a written record from Doctor A's office that might be handwritten and illegible. In addition, the records will all be composed of common, uniform templates and forms, so nothing would be foreign or confusing as it is now.

The record will be complete, not only of Doctor A's treatment, but *every other doctor* Patient A has ever seen. The history and physical will be an on-going collection of the history of this patient. Each visit with each doctor updates the diagnostic codes for which Patient A has been treated in the past and a notation in the History and Physical will have been made. The record is complete and easy to read. It saves time and money, and makes the doctor's job infinitely easier. Doctor B's defensive practices can be tamed to a certain extent because he now has access to all the laboratory work and imaging that was done before. Only necessary tests are ordered according to a standardized health care plan for the individual diagnostic codes generated by the patient. With standardized algorithms of care, the doctors who stay within the written standard of care would not be worried about lawsuits, and the exchange of medical records would provide the necessary transparency of information for health care providers.

If, a year or two later, Patient A goes back to Doctor A and Hospital A, the process is repeated without excessive or entrepreneurial costs because the doctors have access to the common digital record, and what they can do is limited by standard practices. The current doctor will be able to pick up the care without repetition of the raft of tests that occurred in the former scenario.

Costs are cut tremendously because everyone is in touch with the status of the patient at all times. No unnecessary tests are ordered.

PATIENTS' QUALMS AND DOCTORS' OBJECTIONS

The reader, and particularly doctors who might be reading this, might have questions about the digital medical record I have been referring to. There is the ever-present worry about the computer hacker breaking into a database and stealing medical record information, but they would most likely be more interested in the patient's social security number, address, and any financial information than what Patient A was being treated for. The medical information is virtually worthless financially, and the penalties for exposing it are high. For that matter, a simple burglary of a doctor's office and theft of a computer could result in a similar exposure in today's situation.

AN EXAMPLE OF A GOOD MEDICAL RECORD PROGRAM

I have discovered a very nice company in California with an online program that is a model for what I feel could be the answer to the problem at hand. At the time (four years ago) when Medicare/Medicaid was pressuring doctors' offices to develop an electronic medical record, I searched for a record keeping program that might be affordable and adaptable in my own office. I looked at over twenty programs. There are many nice programs out there, but the average cost of these programs was between $30,000 and $50,000, which is prohibitive for small and solo practices. I certainly could not entertain those costs. The cheapest out-of-the-box (OOTB) program that I found usable cost $32,000. Nonetheless, I had to have an EMR or perish.

I searched the web and found "online" medical records. After reviewing the available programs, I decided on an online medical record program called "LeonardoMD." (The reader can visit their web site at http://www.leonardomd.com to observe what I am about to discuss. A free demonstration disc can be ordered that is very helpful.)

"Online records" means just what it says. The company maintains the program and the database, and my office staff and I access the record from a PC with an internet connection. There are several levels of participation, and the record can be tailored to the needs and ability of each office to pay. We chose the "professional" package in which we get online records and electronic billing. The setup fee was $2500 and it is only $300 per month to use. It can easily be used from multiple locations. The company updates the program for free because they maintain the program. If they come up with an improvement, it is added free of charge. The program contains all the ICD-9 diagnostic codes and the CPT codes the government and insurance companies use for billing purposes, and they are periodically updated free of charge.

Switching to an EMR was a mildly troublesome effort because, after having paper charts for over twenty years, it was a real change to deal with a computer. However, we made the transition, and every month we become more efficient because of it. It has the ability to transfer information electronically from records or billings. I can access my records from anywhere in the world with internet access. If the doctors in my area had e-mail capabilities, any and all of my records could go to their office to be printed out. If they were a LeonardoMD subscriber, they could have access to these records through electronic and coded means.

If all doctors were on a similar type of program, and it was universal across the country, the problem of a common medical record would be solved instantaneously. Ten billion dollars a year in taxes is not necessary. The system is already in place. The only thing that would need to be created would be the common templates to make it uniform.

The comparison of this program to OOTB [out-of-the-box]-type programs is very much in favor of the online record. Once an OOTB program is purchased, it is immediately out of date. If there are any changes in the government processes, an update has to be purchased. The office usually has to purchase an expensive service contract for someone to come out and load the new changes into the program, usually during office hours, tying up the service (LeonardoMD usually updates its program late Saturday night or Sunday morning).

With most of the OOTB programs, I was required to purchase computers from the OOTB Company. By the time the package would have been up and running, the cost of the entire program would have been over $45,000. With the LeonardoMD program, we could use the computers already present in the office; there is no requirement to buy "their" computers. We are free to purchase anything we want. It even works well with the new Vista OS from Microsoft. I can use LeonardoMD for ten years or more before I even come close to the purchase price of the cheapest OOTB program. The cost savings enabled me to participate with an EMR, and the program is easy to use for my office staff.

I also have a separate computer-dictation software program that dictates right into the notes and it has saved me between $20,000 and $30,000 of dictation transcription costs, as well as allowing me to have an instant record. One can easily see how the costs are already reduced. Even though I have exceptional handwriting for a doctor, there is no loss of information because of the occasional illegible word or phrase.

It is an extremely easy program to use and it is adaptable to individual preferences. There are a few things I think could be added to the program to make it easier for my office to work faster, and there is a service they perform at no cost that allows anyone to submit a suggestion. Since I have been with the company, many of these suggestions have been implemented, and are very helpful. The price is right as modifications are undertaken free. I cannot think of another situation that could be better. I do feel this is the model to look at to solve the problem of a common digital EMR.

A BETTER WAY

This program could be quickly converted into the common medical record program for the entire country. In the first year (not five years and $50 billion in taxes Mr. Obama wants to spend), our corps of doctors could create all the templates to begin the program on a presently operating online system. The templates can be created for use in every doctor's office and hospital. In one year, we could be one-third of the way to completing the initiation of the long awaited universal health care system, four years ahead of Mr. Obama's expensive government medical record system. In addition, there would be no time lost trying to bend and twist every doctor's present EMR to fit into the new government standards. This first step — of having one program that passes the necessary updates to every hospital and medical office without charge — would save billions of dollars.

We have already reached the state of technology where a common digital electronic medical record is more than just possible. America is in last place when compared to other industrialized nations in technology with respect to computerized medical records. Although we are the richest country in the world, we are still creating medical records like they did in Colonial Williamsburg over two centuries ago.

Summary

To summarize, several things must be brought under control if we are to cut costs and improve efficiency. Defensive, repetitive, and entrepreneurial medicine must be eliminated if we are ever to bring costs down. The common medical record is the easiest step in the process. Let us adopt the online model and energize our doctor corps to make the templates that will allow them to do their job efficiently and cost effectively. Insurance companies need to come under strict regulation. Step I will be to create that system that brings all providers into its utilization. Currently, it is possible to create the common record using present-day technology that is already operational without the taxpayers paying one red cent.

Chapter Nine

STEP II-A:
THE PROBLEM WITH "STANDARD OF CARE"
AND LIABILITY PREMIUMS

THE SECOND problem — and probably the largest wasteful expense — is liability in American health care.

MEDICAL MISTAKES AND LIABILITY

I would be remiss if I tried to tell you that mistakes are not made in the care of patients. Some of these result in serious personal injury or death. Some of these problems are not the fault of the doctor or out of the standard of care. This is the litmus test that is supposed to be used if litigation results. Doctors should not bear the liability of unavoidable adverse outcomes. However, at the same time, the public should have some protection and recourse should they experience one of these unfortunate calamities.

To gain control of liability, we must bear in mind that the present system provides protections to the patient, and in no way should we change the system without maintaining that protection for the patient. In this and the following chapters, we will outline a program that will not only protect the patient but will actually work to improve the standard of care and reduce the number of mistakes. Liability will be handled differently, but the patient will not be forced to forfeit the protection they deserve.

Presently, the recourse is lawsuits against doctors and hospitals for *anything* that goes awry. It is neither right nor fair to blame providers for everything that happens, but they are forced to carry insurance policies to *cover the entire liability*. The courts have bent over backward to make sure patients can exercise their rights. Recent statistics from my own liability insurance plan indicate that the plaintiffs in such cases lose in court 94% of the time, indicating that there is actually less malpractice than the public might surmise. The figure I have always respected throughout my career is that there is approximately 5% true malpractice emanating from true out-of-standard care in America. It turns out my intuition is correct.

Statistics from the Premium Group in Ohio report that greater than 60% of malpractice suits filed are withdrawn. This shows that nearly two-thirds of the suits are not valid and represent an attempt by trial lawyers to "milk" the system, or scare some doctor or insurance company into an early settlement that may not pay millions but could result in several thousand dollars in payouts without a lot of work on the part of the lawyer. Until just a few years ago, this was a valid strategy, but the liability insurance companies have begun to take a hard line and have chosen to fight every claim, no matter what, unless the claim is so obvious there is no defense.

The fact that nearly two-thirds of the cases are withdrawn means that one-third of the cases have at least some merit, but there is only roughly one chance in twelve that a favorable plaintiff verdict will result. Many of these cases could be eliminated by the judge, but it is an extremely rare occurrence.

Summarizing, out of all the cases that are filed, only 5 to 6% result in a win for the plaintiffs and the malpractice lawyers. The Ohio State Medical Association has estimated that it takes an average of $30,000 just to answer each claim filed. The doctor's liability insurance company has lawyers on retainer. Their fees represent a huge cost just to answer the complaint in the court. Most of the cases that are withdrawn without going to court result in expenditures of *at least* $30,000 per case, per doctor involved. The other one-third of the cases also have costs totaling at least that much, and even more, because they require more funds to actually defend in court.

This results in two expensive problems. In reality, 94 to 95% of cases end up having no legal merit in the long run, but the money to defend them has to be spent anyway. Second, we are seeing ridiculous awards from some juries as a "punishment" to the bad doctors for their malpractice. Statistics from the Premium Group show awards as high as $269 million in one case. As much as I value life, and while I maintain a healthy respect for the courts, I do not know of anyone whose life is worth $269 million. This is entirely out of bounds.

What this means is that we are incurring huge costs for about 5% of the actual problems. There is a better way to handle liability.

A CRISIS IN MALPRACTICE OR IN MALPRACTICE PREMIUMS?

A few years ago, I viewed the malpractice hearings on Capitol Hill that are run by Rep. John Conyers (D-MI) nearly every year. This is a well-meaning symposium, but it is rather one-sided on behalf of plaintiffs. Nonetheless, it is an attempt to try to figure out a solution to the problem of medical mistakes, and the effort is commendable. Many cases were presented and truly, some tragedies occurred. Graphic pictures and heart-breaking stories accompanied these presentations.

The message I inferred from the hearings was that, yes, there are medical mistakes in America that result in true human tragedy. These mistakes are mostly preventable, but not all that I saw was the sole fault of the treating physicians. If we apply the above statistics to the meeting, then really these cherry-picked cases represented the worst of the bunch, and a fair representation of the problem was not actually presented.

One of the points brought out at the hearings was that the insurance industry was claiming there is a malpractice crisis in America that is driving our doctors out of business. They were claiming that they could not continue to provide insurance to doctors unless some protection is built into the system. The Bush Administration promoted caps on rewards to try to salvage our resource of doctors, as many physicians have been forced out of business because of increasing liability insurance premiums. This hearing was an attempt to balance that claim with the fact that there is a problem with malpractice in America. In reality, the problem is a two-headed dragon that is disabling the American health care industry with exorbitant costs.

At this same meeting, there was a wonderful discussion by a man named Robert Hunter from the Consumer Federation of America, who gave a presentation with statistics, which clearly proved that there is no true malpractice crisis in America. There is only a crisis in *doctors' premiums* and there has *always* only been a periodic crisis in doctors' premiums. His statistics, collected over thirty years, showed that the amount of payouts for malpractice losses has not risen (as contended by the insurance industry); rather, they have remained static in inflation-adjusted dollars.

His graph is reproduced here and shows direct losses paid per doctor against direct premiums written per doctors (in 2003 dollars).

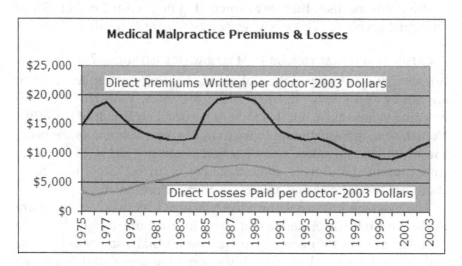

As one can clearly see, the losses in malpractice claims have remained static for thirty years. The graph shows that the only crises that existed have been in the premiums that doctors have had to shoulder.

In the past, doctors simply raised their office prices to offset their increased costs, as any business would do. But the squeeze by the government and insurance companies on the doctors' reimbursements has resulted in a real-life crisis for the doctors because their expenses have outpaced their ability to pay for them. To my knowledge, this has never happened in the history of the country. The government has never sponsored an attack on a private industry's income and stood by while insurance companies have done the same thing to the extent that it has caused the widespread failures of medical practices. All this occurs as insurance companies record profits that make the oil industry look miniscule.

There is overwhelming evidence that a true crisis in malpractice *premiums* does exist. Doctors cannot get hospital privileges without insurance, and there is little significant disparity between the premiums of different companies. The doctors are caught in a huge vice. There is nowhere to turn. The government looks the other way while record profits are made by the owners and investors in medical liability companies. Until there is a real calamity, this is only going to continue.

In the May 2008 issue of *AAOS Now,* in an article entitled, *"Issues facing America: Medical Liability Reform,"* the following statistics were presented.

- **46%**: Percentage of compensation that actually goes to the plaintiff in a medical liability case, after litigation and lawyer's fees
- **$126 billion**: Cost to the already overburdened US health care system related to medical liability in 2002.
- **Five years**: Average time between a medical injury and settlement of a medical liability lawsuit.
- **57%**: Proportion of orthopedists who avoid caring for high-risk patients for fear of liability repercussion (the highest of all specialties surveyed).
- **920%**: Average percentage increase in medical liability premiums from 1976 to 2002.

So-called "Tort Reform"

Several state legislatures have passed laws — called "Tort Reform" — in an attempt to limit awards. Once again, the Premium Group in 2003 (backed up by the Ohio State Medical Association) presented statistics to me in an interview that, in twenty-five states that passed caps on awards through tort reform, liability insurance companies raised their rates to monumental levels until just before the laws were passed. To try to bully the legislation through, the liability insurance companies threatened to stop providing the necessary protection for the doctors by exiting the states, leaving the doctors without insurance. Once the laws passed, the *premiums never returned to the pre-crisis levels*. The rates for family doctors hovered between $30,000 and $50,000 per year. Surgeons were tagged with rates between $75,000 and $130,000 per year.

The one thing the reader must understand here is that tort reform is only as good as the judges who sit on the appellate courts and the Supreme Courts of the states and federal government. In Ohio, tort reform laws have been overturned four times previously, as the legal profession in Ohio took steps to protect their turf.

A new "tort reform" law took place in Ohio April 7, 2005. The Ohio Supreme Court has recently been dominated by conservative judges, as doctors took to the streets to inform the voters that if the conservative judges were not elected, then Ohio risked an exodus of doctors from the state, resulting in a severe crisis. The conservative judges were elected in two successive elections and things in Ohio have stabilized, with malpractice insurance rates beginning to come down to about two-thirds of what they were raised to. However, based on what doctors are paying in many other states, Ohio doctors are still being devastated by high malpractice insurance rates.

In the last election, the conservative balance in the Ohio Supreme Court was not overturned. It is highly unlikely the court will be inundated with lawsuits challenging the tort reform laws in Ohio. This only goes to show that the approach taken by politicians to try to limit out-of-control lawyers is only as good as who sits on the court.

SURGEONS' FEES

In 2006, I attempted to start an insurance company to introduce my new plan. I sought to bring in a consultant/partner, who was the former president of a large health care insurance company. During our discussions, we broached many subjects. One of these regarded the insultingly low fees for my services I was being paid by his former company. He proudly announced that his former insurance company pays $1000 to a surgeon to replace a knee. His argument was thwarted when I informed him that I would have to perform eighty-eight total knee replacements in one year just to pay my malpractice premiums. The average orthopedic surgeon in this country does fourteen knee replacements in a year. I am fortunate to still be able to perform between thirty and fifty a year, but the numbers are falling, and I still cannot cover my liability insurance costs in that manner. Without the ability to raise prices like any other business in America, doctors like me teeter on financial collapse every month.

Recently, the CMS has sought to pay surgeons $600 and less for a total knee replacement. They have put out threats that because of the SGR (Sustainable Growth Rate) formula, they will have to make massive cuts in total joint replacement reimbursements in the next decade. This premise is insulting to doctors when the CMS reimburses the company that makes the total joint prosthesis itself between $2500 and $3500, but they want to pay a surgeon less than it takes to have four tires rotated to use their surgical skills and help someone walk again.

LIABILITY INSURANCE PREMIUMS

Liability insurance companies seek to push doctors to the limit with premiums priced to what the market will bear. In the regular business community, these tactics are useful. In the medical world, however, doctors suffer from a special problem because, in an atmosphere of recently rising runaway jury awards, they cannot practice without the insurance that would protect them. When the rates go up, there is no way to balance it out.

Over a two-year period ending on January 1, 2003, my personal liability premiums jumped from $11,000 to $88,000 a year. There has never been such a jump in premiums in the history of our country. With no losses in over twenty-five years of practice, I am still searching for a reasonable explanation why a surgeon with that kind of record should have to sustain that kind of increase in liability expenses. When I looked on the Internet, the president of my liability company is taking an eight-figure multimillion dollar salary.

Other surgeons and physicians are in the same boat. If one case is filed against a surgeon that results in the routine $30,000 needed to defend it, whether it was valid or not, it could result in an elevation in premiums that would be beyond the ability of the practice to pay for it. This can result in the failure of the practice and a good doctor being put out of business — and it does happen.

A HIDDEN PROBLEM: FEWER QUALIFIED STUDENTS ARE APPLYING TO MEDICAL SCHOOLS

We have already witnessed monumental losses of physicians either quitting practice or retiring early, but there is another hidden problem, which is seemingly going unnoticed — our best students are no longer seeking to enter medicine as a profession in the numbers necessary to maintain the high quality of America's doctors. The effect of this is that during the 2007 Super Bowl, two medical schools were advertising for students on the television in my local area. This would give the impression that the profession has fallen to such a low that reputable schools are seemingly so desperate for competent students that they have to resort to advertising. They are not desperate for applications, but they are desperate for students who are capable of learning the profession and passing the rigid board exams.

A few years ago, I started to write a book named *The Scare Crow Syndrome* about the diminishing skills of people trained in our secondary schools and colleges. In *The Wizard of Oz*, when the Scare Crow asked for a brain, he was told he did not need a brain; he only needed a diploma. Once he was given a diploma, he began to spew forth mathematical formulas. What a fantasy. It made for a good story. In today's world, the reader should try examining some of the applications for employment and witness the atrocious spelling and grammar skills that people exhibit when applying for a job. One could argue that there is a legitimate question as to the general level of training in our preparatory schools.

Furthermore, in my home state of Ohio, colleges have allowed students to stay in school if their GPA falls below an unbelievable level. When I was in college, a student had to maintain a GPA of 2.0 (C) just to stay in school. The school I graduated from still maintains that if a student's GPA falls below 2.0 for two or more quarters or semesters, the student has "flunked out." However, one major state university has now adopted a policy that if a student falls below a cumulative average of 0.5 (D-) in the first semester, they can remain in school. In another state university, students with less than a 1.0 GPA (D) may be dismissed after the first year. While this represents just a minute portion of the broad spectrum of higher education in America, it is a sad commentary on education in America.

The above raises several questions concerning postgraduate studies. A question might be "'What is the real meaning of our "best students?" Is the level of our primary and secondary schools really this bad? Does it mean that currently, even our "best" students are not adequately prepared for higher studies? Or does it mean that our colleges have turned into moneymaking institutions rather than institutions of higher learning, and that they will do anything to keep the tuition dollars flowing?

Tamar Lewin reported in the New York Times on August 17, 2005: "Only about half of this year's high school graduates have the reading skills they need to succeed in college, and even fewer are prepared for college-level science and math courses, according to a yearly report from ACT, which produces one of the nation's leading college admissions tests." In addition, Lewin wrote, "Among those who took the 2005 test, only 51 percent achieved the benchmark in reading, 26 percent in science, and 41 percent in math; the figure for English was 68 percent."

The reader should recognize that math, reading, science and English are actually the core subjects to prepare for medical school. If only half of those entering college can meet the benchmark for these core studies, what does that say about those who did? If the preparation for college has slipped to these dismal levels, even our brightest students may not have the level of preparation needed for their further studies. Perhaps this is because the primary schools are forced to pass students just to graduate enough numbers so as not to attract attention to their failure to educate.

I can remember President H.W. Bush pounding his fist on a podium during a speech. His remark was "we have to graduate more people from high school!" With all that we now know, perhaps his comment might have better served his purpose if he had remarked that we have to do a better job of educating people so they can graduate. I guess, after all, we really do not need a brain; we only need a diploma.

I do not want it to appear that I disrespect my medical colleagues — I have not seen overt signs of gross incompetence. However, the rising numbers of medical "mistakes" does seem to raise a red flag. One needs to ask if the testing standards present several decades ago are still as strict today. A couple of years ago, I stumbled onto a rumor that close to 30% of the graduates of a reputable medical school failed in Part I of the Federal National Board Examinations. Statistics from the USMLE (United States Medical Licensure Examination) indicated that, in 2006 and 2007 those participants from an MD degree school had 7% failures in each year, while those participants from DO degree schools failed at 24% and 19% respectively. These statistics add up to an average of close to 30%. These results contained scores from both first time takers and repeaters. I was unable to find the statistics from the years I took the three parts of the examination.

Unscientific as it is, I do not remember any failures in my own medical school class more than thirty years ago. The public should take comfort in the fact that it is still true that if one cannot pass the test, they cannot secure a license to practice medicine; thus, my own experience with my colleagues and the general level of competence being seemingly safe. However, one does need to ponder if the testing has been made easier to meet the needs of society, or is the system so impossible to work within that it overwhelms our practitioners?

If this *is* true, are we not compounding our liability problem for the future by admitting lesser-qualified students into the profession? Either we have somehow to find a way to attract the best students to the profession again or we *will* have to lower our standards just to get "doctors" into the system.

Career nurses with decades of experience have remarked to me that, in their opinion, comparing the quality of doctors who are ending their careers with what we are seeing today, there has clearly been a change. Because of the lower pay standards, the debt incurred in attaining a medical degree, the length of time it takes to be able to enter practice, and the oppressive liability system in this country, one can make an argument that the better students in college are opting for other lucrative professions, such as engineering, finance, and law. While it is somewhat elitist to broach the subject in this way, most people that I know would rather have the smartest student in the class as their doctor. Right now, no one is really sure that is happening.

So, what can we do?

How do we correct the problems that seem to be occurring in the medical profession in this country? Lawyers have said that if doctors practiced better medicine, there would be fewer suits, and they are partially right. However, the problem is so complex that a simple solution is unlikely.

The first place to start is simply to stop the bleeding. With only 5% of the cases being won by plaintiffs, true liability needs to be redefined. Once that is settled, then a solution to guide our doctors into better and safer practices can be constructed that should improve our situation overall. Systems like the one in Indiana, with tort courts and pre-suit reviews, have improved that state's situation, but further refinement could offer a program that might solve even more of the problems.

Let us build our model by returning to the premise of Robert Hunter of the Consumer Federation of America. Unless the statistics were incorrect, he unequivocally proved that there has been no crisis in malpractice payouts for the past thirty years. From the Premium Group in Ohio, there were an estimated $73 million in losses in 2003. That represented the money that was spent paying all the plaintiffs, attorneys, and court costs. According to Mr. Hunter, dollar per dollar, the same amount of losses occurred in 1973. So, over the past thirty years, if the losses were roughly the same, the losses could be treated as a fixed cost. Once there is a fixed cost, then there are ways to engineer how to pay for that cost, just as any business would do.

To give an example of how easy it is to define the individual risk, consider this. In Ohio, there are roughly eleven and a half million people. If the losses were all that anybody cares about, then it would be a simple task to spread the risk over every person in the state. If one divides $73 million in losses by the eleven and half million people in the state, then it would cost every individual in the state approximately $6 per year to cover all the losses. That is a figure no one can argue with. Even if the losses doubled or tripled for the state, the average person — even someone on welfare — could not offer a plausible argument why they could not afford $6 or $12 or $18 in a year, and that would cover them, no matter how many doctors they visited. So why are we driving doctors out of business with liability premiums approaching $100,000 per year? This example shows that the public could provide coverage for every citizen in the state for just $6 per year. If there were a way to reduce the cost of the attorneys, the costs would drop further.

The above represents all the losses, including attorney fees. The awards that were granted were done without any written standards controlling the doctors' practices. We have no way to know if this represented true out-of-the-standard of care or just the result of some slick attorney arousing a jury.

This new system will put an end to all the questions, and the cost of medical care will go down accordingly. While doctors would still have to purchase a policy to protect them if they make a bone-headed error, they would not have to bankrupt themselves to purchase appropriately priced insurance. Liability insurance companies and some lawyers would see a decrease in their income, but the public will be better because of it, and that is the goal we should all be seeking intently.

The above clearly illustrates an important premise. If the costs of the program are spread across an entire population, they are very small in proportion to what doctors are being charged. If their true liability is only 5%, why are the doctors saddled with the costs for all the liability, with no relief in handling the unethical and unfair rise in premiums as their reimbursements continue to fall? On the other hand, why is there no form of punishment for lawyers and plaintiffs who file frivolous suits? Why do the plaintiffs never have to pay for the legal costs of the defendants as they do in Great Britain and other industrialized countries?

Doctors have been screaming for decades that they are held to a hardly attainable standard. If a plumber messes up your toilet, he generally is not dragged into court and, if he is, his jury is truly a jury of his peers. Generally, he does not have to carry excessively expensive liability insurance to perform his livelihood. Doctors are not allowed any maneuvering room. In fact, malpractice attorneys are constantly bombarding the airways with commercials that alert the public, "If you even think your doctor has made an error, just contact us. We will get you (and us) money." I have yet to see attorney groups advertising on TV seeking to sue a plumber because the toilet does not work. The entire system is like a lottery with people dreaming of hitting the jackpot if the least little thing goes wrong.

WHAT ACTUALLY HAPPENS IN A MALPRACTICE ACTION?

Let us forget all the costs, the depositions, the trial preparations, and examine what actually happens in a malpractice action. It really boils down to who has the better dog-and-pony-show in front of a non-professional jury.

Doctors have a major complaint that they are not afforded the same protection under the law that the general public enjoys. Our legal system guarantees a trial by a jury of our peers, but juries are *not* made up of doctors. Juries are usually made up of everyday, average citizens with only a layman's knowledge of medicine. Doctors have on the average, fifteen years of education after high school to be able to enter the profession. Juries get a week to try to understand the intricacies of a medical case based on what they hear in a courtroom to render a verdict.

No one will seat a jury made up of doctors because the public is convinced by the legal profession that doctors will protect doctors, but nothing could be further from the truth. Doctors are frequently more critical of their colleagues in peer review as they react with the education to do so.

Let us get back to the dog-and-pony-show of the courtroom. The verdict rests in the hands of the expert witnesses. Every state has statutes that require someone who is an "expert" to provide professional testimony to try to persuade or dissuade the jury that the doctor acted *outside of the standard of care* — that he/she actually did something wrong. In the case of malpractice, this means that the doctor took action that a reasonably prudent doctor would not ordinarily do. In the case of the surgeon who amputates the wrong leg, it does not take much education to understand that he made a mistake, but others involve extremely complicated cases with exceptionally involved physiological circumstances that may only happen once in a lifetime. Who is at fault in that case? What about the poor California urologist who removed the wrong kidney when the X-ray technician mislabeled the X-ray films from right to left? The jury said it was the doctor's fault for not recognizing the error on the films. What about the unfortunate eye surgeon in the Pacific Northwest who paid for the training of a technician to calibrate the Lasik machine. The calibration was done incorrectly, and some patients were left virtually blind in the treated eyes. Does a doctor have to check *every detail* in the treatment of patients, including exceedingly complex issues of increasing technology, or should the people who made the error be forced to shoulder the blame? In today's system, the doctor almost always gets sued.

In any event, the argument is to show how the doctor in question did or did not do what a reasonably competent physician should have done. The team of lawyers and expert witnesses that succeed in pleasing the jury wins. Enter a famous attorney who has become nationally prominent. This man successfully charmed juries in his home state into believing that cerebral palsy was a birth injury, which has since been proven scientifically untrue. Entrepreneurial doctors provided testimony that the plaintiff's cerebral palsy was the fault of the delivering obstetrician. These are highly emotional trials with the mother crying on the stand, a sight that one would have great difficulty not feeling something for her loss.

Nonetheless, the experts are paid huge sums of money to testify against good doctors who deliver babies with faulty development mechanisms, not birth injuries. They claimed the obstetricians had failed to uphold the "standard of care." Including medical school, I have been in the profession for thirty-four years, and I have yet to witness any written standard of care of anything in medicine . . . anywhere. The status of the case rests on who can convince the jury just what the (unwritten) "standard of care" is.

The standard of care talked about in the courtroom does not necessarily represent the standard that everyone practices. It represents the opinion that twelve people, or whatever the state requires for juries, say it is. It is based on statements by people who are paid (usually five figures) for their testimony. There are doctors who operate cottage industries in which they offer their testimony for hire. Last year, for the first time, my own specialty board, the American Orthopedic Association (AOA), revoked the board certification from two surgeons who had reportedly provided contrived testimony in a trial. Where has this organization been until now?

STANDARD OPERATING PROCEDURES

That same organization has come up with SOP (Standard Operating Procedures) for expert testimony. I reproduce some of their SOPs here so the reader can learn just what the standard of care is supposed to be.

No. 3: *An Orthopedic expert witness shall evaluate the medical condition and care provided* in light of generally accepted standards *at the time, place and in the context of care delivered.*

No. 4: *An Orthopedic expert witness shall neither condemn performance that falls within* generally accepted practice standards *nor endorse or condone performance that falls outside these standards.*

No. 5: *An Orthopedic expert witness shall state how and why his or her opinion varies from* generally accepted standards.

No. 7: *An Orthopedic expert witness shall* have knowledge and experience about the standard of care *and the available scientific evidence for the condition in question during the relevant time, place and in the context of medical care provided and shall respond accurately to questions about the standard of care and the available scientific evidence.*

No. 12: *An Orthopedic expert witness shall be engaged in the active practice of Orthopedic surgery or demonstrate enough familiarity with present practices to warrant designation as an expert.*

The above represents excerpts of rules by which the profession testifies against members of its own group. I hope the reader realizes that at no time is there a reference in the above made to *a written and accepted standard of care.* There is only a reference to *"generally accepted standards of care at the time, place and in the context of care delivered."* But what is "a generally accepted standard?" Does this not leave the reader with the impression that the standard can change depending upon the circumstances?

"At the time, place, and in the context of care delivered," to me means that the standard can change with respect to the three parameters. How can the standard change? This tells me that the standard does not have to be the same from city to city, state to state, or doctor to doctor. Why would anyone go to court with flexible standards? A procedure is either right or wrong. Either the standard was breached or it was not. There is only one best way to do something. This is the issue so grossly wrong with medical practice. Doctors create their own problems by not maintaining standards that dictate the right way to do something by agreement within their ranks.

In my discussions and focus groups, the one recurring thing that shocks the public is that doctors do not have any written standards by which they practice. There is a characteristic look of horror on the faces of people when they learn that there are only "generally accepted" unwritten standards. Some are furious, others bewildered, as they ponder all of the previous medical care they had undergone in their lifetime. Their horror is well founded. As we ponder the number of medical mistakes that occur, would it be out of the ordinary to postulate that if doctors had a strict code to operate under that many of the problems might just go away?

Where has the so-called "standard of care" been for thirty years?

"THE STANDARDS OF PRACTICE ACT"

When I was a third-year student in medical school at the Bowman Gray School of Medicine of Wake Forest University in Winston-Salem, North Carolina, every student in the class had to prepare a paper for presentation. I chose a topic for my paper that did not represent some facet of clinical medicine but rather a medico-legal theme: "The Standards of Practice Act." In it, I reported that I had observed several doctors treating the same condition differently. Sometimes these treatments were so different that it was difficult to understand how the patient could possibly get better using such different types of care with equal results. My contention was that in a courtroom, there could be no protection if one patient did poorly and the other did better. Why would doctors expose themselves to that kind of risk?

In my paper, I proposed that doctors get together and write rigid standards of care for every diagnostic code they treat. That way, the best way to treat a condition would eventually "float to the top" and medical care would get better over time. In addition, if the standards were defined, then it would be easier for doctors to follow the standards, and it would be difficult to prove to a jury that the treatment given to a patient was outside the standard of care. It would be difficult for an expert witness to come into the courtroom and claim the defendant doctor was out of the standard of care when the doctors created the standards.

When I presented my paper, I was booed and virtually chased out of the room by doctors with venomous expressions on their faces and shouts calling for everything from throwing me out of the room to throwing me out of medical school. No one was more shocked than me to see supposedly smart people turning away something that would provide protection for their patients, as well as themselves. I can still see the chairman of one of the departments, a usually soft spoken and gentlemanly person, pointing his finger at me with hate in his eyes and screaming, "No one is going to tell me how to practice medicine!" I was as shocked by this behavior as the people who have learned that there are still no standards today.

After I was able to gather my ruffled feathers and put the experience in perspective, it became evident what the problem is. There are many jokes about putting a thousand doctors in a room and giving them a problem to solve, and you will be rendered a thousand different opinions and a thousand people willing to fight that their solution is the correct one. It is as if every doctor secretly views himself as better than everyone else around him. That is why it is such a personal tragedy for a doctor to lose a malpractice suit, because what someone is really saying is that he is not the world's top expert he thought he was.

This is a real problem within the ranks of America's medical corps.

It is diffused throughout the entire profession to some degree, and explains how doctors will accept fees for testimony, just to "screw the other guy for a buck." They do this even in the face of statistics that with their contrived testimony, they actually have a 95% chance of raising their own malpractice premiums, as well as the cost of medicine for the entire population.

THE RESULT: DEFENSIVE MEDICINE

This punitive scenario has resulted in doctors practicing defensive medicine. What this entails is that a doctor will go to extensive ends to make sure he has made no mistakes that can come back and bite him in a courtroom. The reader has only to read about the tactics in the courtroom and imagine how it feels to sit in there as a lawyer points at him and exclaims, "If it were not for this bumbling idiot over there who could simply have ordered a $1500 MRI, this problem would have never existed." Those troubles are multiplied many times if there is a death involved, and are escalated off the charts if a baby or a child is involved.

Defensive medicine costs are estimated to account for 25% of the total health care bill in this country. My associate from the insurance industry and I argued over this figure. I told him I am quite sure the figure approaches 50% because I know what I am forced to do in my own practice.

I remind the reader doctors are very much ruled by the premise, "If you think about it – do it." It costs the doctor nothing to write an order for a test or an X-ray or an MRI, but not doing so can be disastrous, not only for the patient but also for the doctor. Even if something goes wrong, a simple letter from an attorney suggesting they are thinking about filing a suit could cause his liability insurance premiums to be raised above what he can afford to pay.

Once again, the only way *any* health care plan is going to succeed rests with its ability to gain control of liability, but currently no health care plan, even President Obama's, addresses liability other than tort reform, which rests on the shaky ground of who sits on the appellate courts. Certainly, none of the health care plans ever presented previously by any candidate for public office does anything other than pay lip service by suggesting tort reform. We might as well install screen doors in submarines.

Step II of this plan will solve that problem and sidestep the complication of the expense of insuring doctors against liability by forcing them to practice in a standardized manner.

"ALGORITHMS OF CARE"

There is already a sort of de facto standardization going on now when insurance companies will not cover certain practices and enact "algorithms of care," not for the betterment of health care but so they can make more money. Certainly, the algorithms set up by the insurance companies do not necessarily benefit the patient. In some cases, they actually force the doctor to *create* a malpractice.

In a health care algorithm, a series of determinations with a path of action that it follows exist. Each "yes" or "no" response directs the doctor onward to another pathway. At the end, there are treatments for each pathway. The algorithm suggests the way a patient should be evaluated and treated.

If doctors do not want people telling them how to practice medicine, then the intelligent thing for them to do is get together and make up the rules themselves. It would be so easy for these intelligent creatures to put together their own algorithms of health care for every diagnostic code we have. This would allow doctors to have some protection from liability and eliminate defensive medicine costs, as well as improve the health care we all desperately need. There *is* really only one right way to do something. Furthermore, as the doctors follow the algorithms, they could have the comfort of knowing they are finally taking the mysticism out of medicine and creating a true science.

THE SYSTEM WILL EVOLVE

I can hear the squeals and arguments coming from the medical professionals already. "Some problems are very complicated," they will say. Yes, gray zones of care exist, but those problems will be dealt with as the program grows, so it would be easy enough to include them within the standard of care. Early on in the process, the standards of care will be necessarily broad for some problems until the review process has a chance to revise them, and strengthen the algorithms through the process of evidence-based medicine.

Naturally, there will be complaints from the legal profession at the thought of dealing with liability other than the traditional way of suing. In this system, no one will be giving up their natural rights. The idea is to tighten the system up so that we have relative assurance that doctors will all be treating patients within appropriate standards. A practitioner can broaden the scope of treatment, but not to ridiculous extremes that puts patients in jeopardy or raises the cost unnecessarily. There will be some regional differences, but basically, the system will evolve naturally and correct itself always toward the betterment of care, which is the argument lawyers always use. If someone is harmed by a truly out-of-the-standard-of-care act, there will still be room for lawsuits, if the patient or family chooses to take that route. No one is forfeiting the right to sue, but by clarifying the standards, everyone wins.

It is not that difficult to formulate standards of care for a profession within which we all work.

DOCTORS WILL START THE PROCESS

Initially, doctors will gather in conference by specialty and set up the standards. The standards will control every action in the treatment of a patient, from initiation of the protocol until discharge, transfer, or consultation. This is a vaunting task, but it is not impossible.

People generally look for written standards to guide our actions in society. For instance, if the police arrest you, there are written protocols they must follow or they are in danger of retribution from the courts for criminal or civil problems. As long as the police stay within the written guidelines, they can exercise their power and will likely win any court case against them. Is it not interesting that the numbers of suits leveled against the police are miniscule compared to the medical profession?

Patients like to believe that if they go to a doctor in one office that there is a standard practice of evaluation and management, that their doctor is doing things correctly, but at present, there is no written and accepted plan for anything except "generally accepted standards of care." In the medical journals, there is the occasional representation of an algorithm, but no written standard forces anyone to follow it.

HOW THE PLAN WILL WORK

This plan will require all doctors in the country to come together to create standards of care for every diagnostic code and virtually everything encompassed in the treatment of a patient. Each year, they will be bound, as part of their continuing medical education requirement to go back into conference and review the previous year's results. At this meeting, in an attempt to better the care, the plans will be adjusted according to the results of treatment.

Boards of inquiry will be set up to review problem cases. The boards will determine one of four things:

1. The care was not out of the standard of care.
2. The care was out of the standard of care.
3. The care resulted in a complication.
4. The care resulted in an adverse outcome.

True "out of the standard of care" can then be referred to the courts, or the plaintiff can accept an agreed-upon sum representative of the injury that occurred.

Each year the system will tighten its grip on the health care standards, and doctors who cannot seem to follow suit will be retrained, placed under strict supervision, or be removed from the system. If they are just bad doctors, they will lose their license and be banned from the profession altogether.

SUMMARY

In summary, medicine is the only area of large public contact that I know of where there are no written standards. These written standards of care will guide the practitioner as the system matures. It will grow to provide protection against liability claims by standardizing care and making doctors practice better medicine. The public will generally respect the effort and lean towards acceptance of the consequences if the doctor is within the written standard of care. It will also eliminate the cottage industry of phony medical experts. If the practice is within the guidelines, there can be no malpractice.

The liability problem is more complex than that however. The vast majority of problems in medicine are not *out of the standard of care* issues. Statistics indicate that only 5 to 6 % of lawsuits have an outcome that goes against the doctor. Most lawsuits emanate from what I refer to as *complications or adverse outcomes*. A calamity can occur in the treatment of someone and have nothing to do with the care the doctor provided. That is either a complication or an adverse outcome.

In the next chapter, we will consider the second part of Step II, *management of complications and adverse outcomes*. Then we will put it all together and see how the program actually improves health care, cuts costs, and allows us to insure everyone for an affordable cost.

Chapter Ten

STEP II-B
MANAGEMENT OF COMPLICATIONS AND ADVERSE OUTCOMES

A s WE stated before, not everything that goes wrong in the treatment of a patient is the result of malpractice or out-of-the-standard of care. The court system provides a protection for the patient. This protection cannot be sacrificed in the search for a better and cheaper way to solve this expensive and cumbersome problem. This chapter will deal with "adverse outcomes" and offer a solution to rationally deal with the problem.

AN ADVERSE OUTCOME

Perhaps I should define what is meant by a complication or an adverse outcome. Both mean that something went wrong and a perfect result did not occur, but the negative outcome is not necessarily the fault of the treating physician.

In fact, most of the lawsuits generated are actually a result of complications and adverse outcomes, and not malpractice; otherwise, there would be a much larger percentage of malpractices losses by defendant providers in the courts. If there is only a 5% chance of actual out-of-the-standard-of-care treatment, then it is unfair to burden physicians with the entire amount of liability. This burden can and should be shared by the patient.

Any medical treatment bears some risk. For the record, I am going to make the statement and stand by it that *there is no way that anyone can legislate or litigate away the risk out of living on this planet.* America has reached breaking point with the cost of health care and the patient is going to have to assume some of the risk. Some medical treatments bear a more significant risk than others do, and while the doctor is bound within medical ethics, and hopefully in the future by rigid written standards of care, no one can guarantee a perfect or even favorable result from *any* treatment. However, in our present system of litigation, we can reasonably guarantee that a standard could be followed. When that standard is indeed breached and some kind of injury results, then there is a way to provide a system of compensation for the patient. Presently that is through the courts and will be maintained. If an injury results that happened within the standards, there is a way to compensate the patient as well.

THE PROBLEM OF COMPLICATIONS AND ADVERSE OUTCOMES

The problem of complications and adverse outcome is a difficult one for the public to grasp. If something goes wrong in their care, the patient almost always recognizes this as something the doctor did incorrectly: something went wrong, so it is someone's fault. That is a capsule summary of medical jurisprudence today.

Any adverse outcome can result in legal action with a lawsuit for malpractice. Where we are failing is that, in all but about 5% of the cases, the adverse outcome of treatment is frequently not the fault of anyone. Taking care of patients is a hugely complicated undertaking. Although most of what we do in medicine is based on a long history of treating patients, the very same treatment in two different patients can often result in two different outcomes.

Therefore, in the scheme of things, one of four things happens to a patient:

1. The desired result is achieved.
2. The desired result is not achieved because of a breach of some vague standard of care.
3. A complication occurs.
4. An adverse outcome occurs.

How the patient views his outcome determines whether consultation with another physician or an attorney occurs. What one patient perceives as an acceptable outcome might not suit another. The plan to be introduced will clarify these outcomes.

An example might help to understand these concepts.

AN EXAMPLE: A COMPLICATION

Let us assume that a patient reports for treatment with painful hips. His hips are completely worn out, and he has some past medical problems that raise the risk of many types of recognized complications.

Patients do not like to hear about the awful things that can happen to them. They are given the warnings and the chance to opt out of the surgery or other treatment. It is explained to the patient that the general risk for death from a total hip is perhaps one in a hundred.

In most hospitals now, there are standardized treatment plans for total joint surgery. These algorithms are called "critical pathways." They are called "critical" because certain of the treatments are critical to the attempt at a good outcome without complications or adverse outcome. They are algorithms for treatment that set up parameters for what medicines are to be used, pre- and post-op testing, and pre- and post-op treatments, such as anticoagulation, pain medicines, antibiotics, and physical therapy.

Every patient undergoing total hip replacement surgery is automatically treated within these parameters, and thus, to a certain extent, the control of the patient is removed from the doctor in favor of these critical pathways. They are meant to aid the doctor so certain aspects of treatment are not inadvertently left out. However, regardless of the attempt to direct the care, things can happen to the patient that are not desired or expected.

We will assume the total hip replacement is done and the patient comes out of the surgery in good shape. Within eight to twelve hours, an anticoagulant (blood thinner) is automatically administered. In our example, on the first post-operative day, our patient develops some calf pain, a duplex scan (Doppler) is run, and a blood clot is detected in the calf. Although the critical pathway automatically had the nurse begin a program of prophylactic doses of a blood thinner within eight to twelve hours of the surgery, the patient developed a blood clot just the same.

Now that a blood clot has been detected, the pathway directs the doctor to increase the level of the blood thinner to a fully anti-coagulated state. Through titration of the medications, the laboratory work eventually confirms that his blood has reached the desired level of anticoagulation.

On the third postoperative day, our patient develops chest pain and is transferred to the CCU (coronary care unit). All of the tests indicate the patient has not had a heart attack and, although his lung scan is clear, he is actually having chest pain because very small fragments of the clot are breaking off and traveling to the lung. Until recently, these "micro emboli" were for the most part undetectable.

On the fourth postoperative day, he develops a pulmonary embolism because a large piece of the blood clot has broken off, traveled to his lung, and clogged it up so no blood can get to the lung. He suffers an immediate death.

Was there a breach of the standard of care in this case? No, the operation was conducted in the prescribed fashion, and the X-rays confirm the surgery was done correctly. The critical pathway was followed by the floor personnel and the patient received the prophylactic blood thinner on time. When it was noticed that calf pain had developed, the appropriate measures were taken to diagnose the blood clot and treat it by increasing the level of anticoagulation by making the blood "thinner." The symptom of chest pain developed and, with a history of two previous cardiac events, the patient was moved to the CCU, where two days later he died of a massive pulmonary embolus.

In our example, the patient was treated with the required steps to prevent a blood clot but, in spite of our efforts, the clot developed anyway; this was a blood clot out of the doctor's control and on appropriate preventative medicines. According to this scenario, the doctor did not act out of the standard of care. The critical pathway was followed to the most critical details, so technically there was no malpractice.

The formation of a blood clot is not malpractice; it is a complication, which the *Merriam Webster Dictionary* defines as "a secondary disease or condition developing in the course of a primary disease or condition." In this instance, the complication resulted in an unwanted or unexpected outcome, even though all of the medical care offered to the patient was appropriate.

A complication does not always result in injury or death, but it may entail further medical treatment to address it. In the case of our hypothetical patient, the doctor followed the appropriate pathway, which represented the true standard of care in that particular location, and he did nothing incorrectly. The blood clot was the complication and the pulmonary embolism was an adverse outcome that resulted in the patient's death. Is it anyone's fault? No. There is no way that this outcome could be predicted, legislated, or litigated out of happening.

Nevertheless, many times an attorney will file a wrongful death suit in a case like this. A judge is unlikely to take the step to review what actually happened and dismiss the case. Judges are more likely to let a jury determine what happened, and whether or not the case has substance, it is thrown into the courts. There is no mechanism to control attorney fees, and huge costs are generated just to answer the claim.

Attorneys' eyes open wide when they get a case in which someone has died because that really gets the attention of a lay jury. The plaintiff attorneys argue that someone died and it has to be someone's fault. If they can create a better dog-and-pony-show than the defense, they stand to win many thousands — if not millions — of dollars.

The above represents a real live case that actually happened. In the end, two family doctors, one internist, two radiologists, and a vascular surgeon were implicated by the accusation as having "acted out of the standard of care." Two of the primary care doctors panicked and settled their cases without going to court, even though the critical pathway was followed. The remaining suits were withdrawn. According to the OSMA(Ohio State Medical Association), each physician incurred a basic cost of about $30,000 just to answer the suit.

Even though the operating surgeon was not implicated in the suit, his insurance company sought the advice of counsel and there was a cost generated for the surgeon as well. Seven doctors' insurance companies had to come up with a total of $210,000 just to answer the suit. All of this was done, even though the standard of care was not breached and was actually followed to the letter. The settlement by the two primary care doctors was unnecessary, as they would have prevailed in the court.

As a result, all of the doctors received "occurrences" on their insurance company record, which meant their malpractice premiums would not be lowered if, and when the time came for that to happen. The attorneys walked away with most of the money, the family was left embittered and without what they felt was their appropriate compensation. This could have all been avoided.

Most "malpractice" is actually "adverse outcome"

Most medical malpractice suits are initiated because of complications and adverse outcomes rather than true out-of-the-standard-of-care. The statistics support this premise. In my own state, over 60% of the malpractice cases are withdrawn without making it to a courtroom. In the remainder of the cases, only 5% result in a loss for the defendant. Those 5% are the true out-of-the-standard of care results in which the court has determined that there was indeed malpractice. The rest of the cases must be attributed to complications and adverse outcome or a frivolous action.

These suits are one of the things that make the overall cost of health care so high. The missing part here is that there are no written standards of care to cover the doctor's practice. The critical pathway is actually an algorithm of care and it is a good start but, in the above example, we have seen that the vagaries of the law allow an attempt on the system that results in a loss even though a written standard existed. An expert witness, who has made a career out of offering testimony against other doctors, can freely come in to a courtroom and instruct the jury that the doctor did something wrong or the patient would still be alive.

The most vivid example of this occurred in the courtrooms where a nationally famous attorney convinced juries that cerebral palsy was the result of a birth injury. He made a lot of money utilizing bogus science and medical experts, who were paid high fees to provide misleading testimony. His performance in the courtroom was legend. Because of his exploits, the number of C-section births in this country skyrocketed, as doctors performed unnecessary C-section operations as extreme defensive medicine techniques in an attempt to avoid litigation based on case law that came out of these bogus lawsuits. This has resulted in the highest cost anywhere in the world to deliver a baby. As a result, many doctors in the US are opting not to deliver babies because of it.

The standard of care in one community must not be allowed to be different from that in another community. A human being in New Mexico is the same as one in Rhode Island. By failing to create a written standard of care and algorithms to follow, doctors have left themselves vulnerable to these types of legal attacks. This creates a huge loophole that allows trial attorneys to create doubt in the minds of the jury.

The adverse outcome does not even have to involve a death; it can be any type of injury. It costs the same to file and answer a lawsuit over a torn fingernail as it does when someone dies. A written standard of care would help to clarify the issue for everyone.

Millions of patients visit doctors' offices every day. Millions of treatment plans initiated every day are ultimately successful. They result in neither complications nor adverse outcomes nor out-of-the-standard care. However, they could. The risk that anyone bears in seeking health care necessarily includes complications and adverse outcomes, and no one is able to predict when the complication or the adverse outcome will occur.

In our legal system today, a complication or an adverse outcome represents 100% chance that a lawsuit can be filed, regardless of whether the patient was treated appropriately. This threat, defensive medicine tactics, and the accompanying repetitive medicine, repeating the same information on the medical records over and over again, is what causes the incredible drain of funds on our health care system.

THE NEW PLAN WILL CALL FOR WRITTEN STANDARDS OF CARE

The new plan will call for written standards of care for every diagnostic code. In today's scheme of medical care, most care plans are initiated by doctors who have developed their own style or approach to that particular problem. Some people refer to it, with a romantic flair, as the art of practicing medicine, but frequently, in the everyday constraints of a busy medical practice, these plans can and do go astray. If this country wants to bring health care costs under control, this type of medicine should be retired forever and some type of doctor-generated controls instituted.

As I have discussed this problem with my focus groups, I have found that the public is overwhelmingly ignorant of the fact that presently there is no true written standard of care for every diagnostic code. This is always left up to the "art" of practicing medicine. Most doctors are very astute, keep reasonably good records and are able to follow a simple care plan that resides in their head.

However, as we have previously seen, one doctor's care plan can be radically different from any other doctor's plan, so it is easy to understand why the same patient can visit several doctors seeking the answer to a health care problem and get several different opinions. Not every mistaken diagnosis leads to a calamity, but it can lead to a lot of medical waste and raise the cost of health care.

IF PILOTS CAN HAVE STANDARD OPERATING PROCEDURES, WHY CAN'T DOCTORS?

The Federal Aviation Administration (FAA) requires professional pilots to follow rigid checklists to prevent airline accidents. Almost every airline calamity can be traced back to a breach of a standard operating procedure. A very slight distraction can lead, even the most competent of flight crews to forfeit their lives, as well as those of their innocent passengers. Most of these pilots are incredibly adept at flying an aircraft; however, a minor distraction or a temporary loss of concentration can be fatal.

If the FAA can institute these procedures and achieve the tremendous safety record we are witnessing, then we certainly can do the same thing in medical care. Granted, it is less complicated to fly an airplane in the air traffic control system than it is to take care of sick people, but it is the approach to the problem that is important here. Without categorizing everything and setting up rules to follow, we are left to the calamities that happen and few ways to defend them should a suit be filed. There is no way to eliminate accidents and injury in aviation, but the number of accidents, injuries and deaths has fallen dramatically. We should be seeking this goal in medical practice. Anything less is a disgrace. America leads the world in technology and computerization. We have the methods and means to employ these powerful tools to take care of patients and make it easier, cheaper and safer to do so.

WHAT WE NEED TO DO IS SET UP ALGORITHMS FOR PATIENT CARE

The Miriam-Webster Online Dictionary defines an algorithm as "a step-by-step problem-solving procedure, especially an established, recursive computational procedure for solving a problem in a finite number of steps." In flying an airplane, the procedures for flying these complex machines constitute a form of an algorithm. Distractions occur, but the algorithms generally keep the aircraft in a safe attitude and under control. The cockpit is a relatively sterile environment. There is the radio communication with air traffic control, and the pilot can get information from the instruments and the co-pilot. It can be a busy time but, with the implementation of standardized procedures, they have been relatively reduced to an algorithm that has escape pathways if a change in the procedure results in an emergency situation, as witnessed by the recent successful water landing in New York City.

A doctor's life, on the other hand, is anything but a sterile environment. During a typical day, the doctor has an unbelievable tug of war for his attention. Everyday a line of patients parades through the office, paying for the attention. The phone rings off the hook. Everyone from other doctors to physical therapists, ward nurses, visiting and hospice nurses, operating rooms, insurance agents, and pharmacists are trying to contact the doctor. Every interruption of the doctor's thought processes opens a pathway for error. If a pilot had to fly an airplane with the number of distractions that doctors face every minute of their day, the country would be littered with crash sites.

ADVERSE OUTCOME SHOULD BE COVERED BY INSURANCE

However, while rigid standards of care might result in lowering true out-of-the-standard-of-care problems, no care plan can protect the public from the routine complications and adverse outcomes of medical treatment. The doctors should bear the burden of providing care that is within a reasonable standard, but they should not have to pay a fortune for insurance to cover injuries that result from unpreventable complications and adverse outcome.

No liability insurance plan presently pays for recognized complications and rightly so, as these mostly natural occurrences happen outside of the doctor's care. However, since millions of care plans are initiated every day, a liability insurance plan could be created that allows the patient to purchase insurance against an adverse outcome.

Since so many of our daily treatments result in successful outcomes, it is a perfect situation for an insurance plan to be successful and provide protection. The vast majority of people who visit doctors and who initiate treatments end up with successful outcomes. Whenever the statistics predict a majority of good results, a perfect situation begins for an insurance company to begin a plan that can compensate those subscribers who have untoward results. This opens the door to revolutionizing the liability system in patient care.

The more people there are in the system, the better the chance of spreading the cost and keeping it down. A larger actuary table has the best chance of keeping the cost down. Since there would be as many as 300 million patients in the system, the insurance protection would be extremely cheap to administer.

Even something as simple as a sore throat could generate a cheap policy that would offer protection. A sore throat is a seemingly simple problem to care for, but serious complications can arise. A sore throat could result in a peri-tonsillar abscess or an epiglotitis that could cut off the windpipe and suffocate the patient. All doctors have seen this happen or have heard of it. Overall, a sore throat is not likely to injure or kill a patient, but it could. With three hundred million people in the system, the per-person insurance premium to protect against all the complications and adverse outcome from treatment of sore throats across the country would perhaps be $1. If everyone got a sore throat, that $1 premium would put $300 million in a reserve fund just to solve complications and adverse outcome from sore throats. People infrequently have more than one diagnostic code generated per year. Some people always seem to be at the doctor's office and others never seem to go. Nonetheless, with the overwhelming number of successful outcomes of treatment daily and with the small amount it would cost to insure oneself against serious complications and adverse outcome, there would be more than enough reserve to cover the risk, as well as build a reserve to help people with premiums that lose their jobs. The risk would be spread across the population and no one will go broke paying for it. Once again, we see that spreading the cost over the entire population makes it affordable for us all.

USING A COMPUTER TO HELP DIAGNOSE A PROBLEM

Taking care of a patient is obviously not like fixing a starting problem in a car engine. Each patient gives a different version of their history and defines their discomfort in a different fashion. Trying to decode the messages can lead one on the path to misdiagnosis, resulting in higher costs when the diagnosis comes out incorrect. I have read reports that a doctor's ability to reach the correct diagnosis within the differential diagnosis on first contact is somewhere around 15%.

In November, 2006, a British firm, dailymail.co.uk, reported impressive results when doctors used the Google search engine to try to diagnose medical problems, and the result was that 58% of the diagnoses in a list called differential diagnosis were correct on the first try.

Dailymail.co.uk suggested doctors must treat patients by carrying as many as 2 million medical facts in their brains. They reported studies of autopsies showed that doctors misdiagnosed fatal illnesses 20 percent of the time. As medical knowledge expands, doctors necessarily must find ways to keep up. Doctors that are adept at using Google fared very well in diagnosing difficult cases. A computer memory is not affected by interruptions, distractions, telephone calls, aging, and so on, in the way a human is.

I experimented with this process and found that I am very comfortable using the computer to aid in my diagnostic effort. I found that my diagnostic accuracy improved by simply typing the symptoms into the search engine and returning a rough differential diagnosis. I like to think I am a pretty competent physician, but I was surprised to see the number of entities that my brain had eliminated by just not having come into contact with them since medical school or even just a decade ago. I was delighted to see how simple it was to initiate the process with a larger differential diagnosis. It made for a more practical search for my answer, and combining my training, experience, and physical skills with what I found online made me a better doctor. It also increased the speed at which I was able to arrive at the correct diagnosis and proceed with the treatment. I cut down many steps in my process, and I am quite sure I saved money doing it.

Granted, there are doctors in the world with greater brainpower. Every doctor would like to aspire to have the diagnostic skills of the mythical title character on the TV show "House." That, however, is not realistic, as that character is easily written to make it look like he is a Cray Supercomputer in a white coat. While there may be a few people like him in real life, the vast majority of doctors have good skills and they are very bright, but they are not the superstars of intellectual capacity that "House" represents.

In this day of overworked and understaffed, distracted and fatigued physicians, why not take advantage of the greatest tool ever invented — the computer. By setting up a care plan for every type of problem we face, and combining that with the diagnostic capabilities of the highly trained doctor with the memory capabilities of the computer, we could have the answer to solving the medical crisis we face in this country.

Just as I had suggested thirty years ago in medical school, the standards of care would be set for every diagnostic code we have and the treatment would be established. If a doctor had a way to follow a care plan for each and every patient, then ventures outside of the standard of care, as well as complications and adverse outcomes should decrease. There would also be a way to track everything that happened to the patient and potentially head off errors in diagnosis and treatment. In addition, there would be ways to control entrepreneurial behavior, and keep physicians and other providers on the straight and narrow.

COMPUTERIZED CARE ALGORITHMS WILL LOWER THE COSTS OF CARE

By using algorithms, we would have a pathway that everyone in the country would be forced to use, standardizing care across the board. There would no longer be a local standard of care that is "generally accepted" and different from the standard in other communities.

Without an algorithm as a guide for the standard of care, the doctor could elect a defensive medicine posture, and just initiate a plan of care that is expensive even being done purely to make money. With either a defensive medicine posture or the entrepreneurial posture, in the current medical system, charges are initiated for those patients that might be unnecessary. In one case, the doctor is paid for his defensive tactics. In the other, he is paid just because he can institute the treatment for the sole purpose of making money. In the case of the patient who does not need the treatment, his bill goes up unnecessarily. In the event there is an adverse outcome from just performing the test or treatment for defensive purposes or entrepreneurial purposes, then that opens up another whole issue for the system to endure.

One can readily see that the lack of a written standard can lead to an expert witness being hired to testify in one way if patient, for example, did not get drugs and ended up getting a blood clot, and in another way, if there were a complication of using the drugs. However, if the diagnostic code group for the symptoms presented by the patient had a written standard, there would be no need for defensive medicine because the written standard would cover the doctor's action. If something adverse came of the treatment, the doctor would be within the standard of care, and the patient would be covered by other forms of insurance, not just lawsuits.

The computerized system would list diagnostic (ICD-9) codes for diagnosis and (CPT) codes for payment at each stage of the algorithm. This computerized clinical pathway allows for tracking of treatments by every doctor in everything he does. If he follows the prescribed treatment plans, then he is paid exactly as he should be paid. If the doctor tries to violate the protocol and just go to the treatment and payment portion of the algorithm, the computers would pick up the violation in treatment and not allow payment or treatment unless there was some built-in appeal mechanism or some other such way to change the protocol legitimately.

In this system, no defensive, repetitive, or entrepreneurial medicine would be allowed. The cost would come down but the doctor would still maintain protection if an adverse outcome should result. He is not paid if he is not supposed to be, and he is not sued if he stays within the agreed upon guidelines.

Computerizing these treatment plans also allows for easy tracking of physician behavior, as well as compliance by the patient.

Obviously, there are going to be some gray areas that are going to have to be worked out. Some of the treatment patterns become complicated in the case of multi-system involvement; that is, if several different body systems are involved in a critically sick or injured patient. In that case, the status of the patient will have to enter into the equation because the physical status does have a direct correlation with outcome: the sicker the patient, the more likely a less than perfect outcome. We must offer some protection to the doctors who are tasked with the medical care of these more difficult and sicker patients.

HEALTH INSURANCE POLICIES UNDER THIS PLAN

In the proposed plan, the cost of the policies that protect against complications and adverse outcomes would be so cheap that no sensible person would dare go without one. However, one could still opt out of the policy by signing an agreement that the insurance was being rejected, similar to what one does when one chooses not to buy the insurance on a rental car.

There will be a statement that one is of sound mind, is rejecting payment of the insurance fee, and will accept the responsibility and the liability of adverse outcomes completely. If an adverse outcome occurs, then no money would pass hands and the issue would be settled.

The beauty of this policy is that one's life has a reasonable value placed on it and if major adverse outcome occurs, the payment is immediate. No one has to engage an attorney. No one has to share the winnings. No one has to wait five years to get into a court. There would be no 94% chance of failure. The insurance would be there to protect against the adverse outcome because, under the new system, if the doctors stayed within the written and agreed-upon standard of care, there could be no claim of malpractice.

Doctors will have to decide what represents a recognized complication and what represents adverse outcome for each diagnostic code. A panel made up of lay citizens, doctors, and insurance personnel could set the prices on what is paid out for loss of limb and life. As the system matures, those costs would be more realistically adjusted and appropriate reserves would be kept for times when higher rates of adverse outcome occur.

While there would be no more eight-to-ten-figure awards, a fair loss of life or limb policy would immediately cover losses. In this system, true malpractice would be clarified in the eyes of the public. True out-of-the-standard of care could be monitored and controlled. The result would ultimately be better medical practice, better outcomes, and fewer injuries.

In reality, no one would be giving up any rights. For true out-of-standard care that occurs in bypassing the written standards that results in injury or death, the patient or family would retain the right to sue if the behavior was deemed malpractice and not a complication or adverse outcome. The expected objection by the legal profession would be negated before it begins. This would help to eliminate the frivolous and unnecessary suits that are adding to all the problems.

CREATING STANDARDS-OF-CARE ALGORITHMS IS THE FIRST STEP

Creating standards-of-care algorithms will not entirely solve the problems with health care in America, but it is the first step in creating this health care plan for the future, and there will be opportunities to revise the standards based on real-world experience to improve care over time. Improved care means fewer missed diagnoses. It means fewer mistakes in treatment. It creates a method to review our records with three hundred million people in the database, and to develop the best evidence-based medicine possible. Better treatment leads to improved outcomes, which will result in fewer liability problems. The whole system will result in better health care — and better health — for all Americans, as well as bringing the costs down to reasonable levels.

With written standards of care, elimination of the expensive defensive medicine strategies employed by doctors in today's market will bring the cost of health care down, in my estimation, by 40 to 50%. This is a huge cost savings! Combining standards of care with elimination of repetitive medicine will further drop the cost to about 60%. This brings the cost of medicine down from $2.2 trillion to just under $1 trillion. This is without even bringing Medicare/Medicaid patients into the fold and losing those huge administrative costs that accompany every government bureaucracy.

Chapter Eleven

STEP II-C
LIABILITY AND THE FORMATION OF A PLAN
TO MANAGE RISK

W E ARE faced with the problem that adverse outcome can be increased in volume and severity based on the condition of the patient when care begins. As a patient's physical condition deteriorates, through either disease or simply poor physical condition, the chance of a complication or adverse outcome necessarily increases. Likewise, the doctor's liability also increases, and that brings along additional costs.

SOME PATIENTS REQUIRE EXTENDED TREATMENT

The standard of care for a healthy person undergoing a treatment or surgery actually changes when other health care issues enter the formula. In my own specialty, a patient who is otherwise healthy but is a cigarette smoker greatly increases the chance that fracture healing will be delayed. This is a very real problem. Necessarily, I have to extend the care of these patients beyond the routine to head off liability problems for myself, as well as to try to get a successful outcome for the patient. Smokers have blamed me for their inability to heal their fractures, and I have had at least one lawsuit by a woman whose leg did not heal because she refused to quit smoking. The lawsuit was withdrawn when the plaintiff could not find an expert to say that my treatment was out of the standard of care, but the occurrence remains on my permanent record.

Extending treatment increases the chance that an adverse outcome will occur, so defensive medicine tactics are initiated. More tests and

X-rays will be necessary to document the progress of an illness or injury clearly. Without them, the condition can take a turn without the doctor knowing it, culminating in a more serious problem that could make it look like the doctor was negligent in his treatment of the patient. This opens up the door for malpractice action.

It takes six to eight weeks for most fractures to achieve a level of strength that allows a patient to return to most activities. A cigarette smoker can extend that to three to six months, and in some cases, until the smoking ceases completely. This means that more X-rays are taken past six weeks, and that a cast or other protective device needs be applied over a longer period of time. This equates to more time off work or more time on limited duty at work for the patient, and that results in increased costs for the employer. Along with all the above, the chance that the fracture will not heal or may need further treatment — including operation, re-operation with bone grafting, bone stimulation, and heavy therapy costs — rises in geometric proportions. This single act of smoking is responsible for billions of health care dollars lost each year, as well as raising the chance that something will go wrong with the care that will result in a disability for the patient and a lawsuit for the provider. After all, something went wrong, so the most likely person to blame is the doctor.

A SYSTEM TO RANK PATIENTS IS NEEDED

For the above reasons, a system is needed in the scheme we have created to rank patients based on their physical and mental status, a system that calculates the risk they raise for complications and adverse outcome.

On the health care recipient side, we are already seeing this addressed, as some employers have initiated payments by the patient to help pay for the increased cost of an insurance plan just because of things like smoking, obesity, diabetes, and the presence of pre-existing illnesses, such as heart disease, HIV, and lung disease. These substantially increase the risk of complications and adverse outcome, as well as generally inflating the cost of caring for more routine illnesses and injuries. In the plan being built here, the insurance costs to cover complications and adverse outcome would be uncontrollable if there were not some kind of ranking system based on the status of the patient.

The American Society of Anesthesiologists has a classification they have used for decades based on the relationship of physical status to anesthetic mortality. A series of categories was developed and it was surprisingly accurate in predicting the risk. Simply put, based on your physical status, you are ranked on the likelihood that you could die under anesthesia. The system is useful in ranking patients with co-morbid conditions that could result in fatality. The greater the number of co-morbid conditions, the higher the rank, because the likelihood of a fatality increases with the poorer physical state of the patient. Anesthesiologists do not consider this as an estimate of operative risk but rather of the patient's condition prior to surgery, and it is used to generate statistical data for anesthesia so there would be a standard for anesthesiologists to discuss cases and their outcomes.

Medical practice is replete with the grading of patients using taxonomic classifications to better facilitate communication between physicians who review results of treatment. The anesthesia rating system was rather vague, and somewhat subjective and intuitive in nature. However, even though it has had its problems, it results in an assessment of risk, which must necessarily be recorded before a procedure is done. Anesthesiologists stand by the adage, "The sicker the patient, the more likely the patient is to die with anesthesia." One might think that that is glaringly obvious, but the technique of ranking patients is incredibly valuable in predicting risk of medical treatment.

The following is the basic physical status ranking system used by some anesthesiologists. It is from a table in a study in the Journal of Anesthesiology, Volume 49, No. 4, October 1978, page 234 from a study by Marx et al. of 34,145 patients. It indicates the surgical mortality as a percent of those people undergoing surgery.

ASA Classification of Physical Risk

Physical Status	% Mortality
PS 1	0.06
PS 2	0.47
PS 3	4.4
PS 4	23.5
PS 5	50.8

One can see that in category 1, there is a very small risk of mortality. Even in classification 3, the risk is only 4.4% in this study. However, there is a big jump in the risk between classifications 3 and 4, as there is between classifications 4 and 5. Clearly, this study shows that as the physical status of the patient deteriorates, the likelihood of dying during the surgical procedure correlates well with the pre-surgical evaluation.

Ranking patients and the likelihood they will develop complications and adverse outcome is a necessary part of this health care plan, but the change that will be instituted with this plan differs from the way managed denial companies do it. They rank patients on the likelihood the patient with co-morbidities will cost them more money so they use co-pays, high deductibles, and simple denial of treatment to try to limit access by those patients to the system. In addition, grouping patients together with co-morbid conditions and then dropping the group is a technique that further increases their profits. Insurance companies seek to sell policies to people who are not sick or not more likely than the norm to become ill. If a person with a particularly clean "bill of health" is in the group that is dropped, he can simply join another group. This is not so for those with health care problems.

The difference between private and government insurance is that the government allows an open door to treatment but they cannot pay for it, so they bundle all of their care under one code and cut the payment to less than what it costs to provide it, and the provider suffers financially. However, even in the face of these controls, the government's system has still overwhelmed the ability of Medicare to pay for services.

In this plan, *all* patients qualify for medical treatment. However, if Americans are, by their own volition, going to continue to smoke cigarettes, have sedentary lifestyles that lead to obesity and diabetes and other diseases plaguing them then they are going to incur a higher ranking. Therefore, they should have to shoulder part of the cost of their own risk, not an increased cost for their care. We are not talking hundreds of dollars here, just the amount the actuary table states will balance the risk.

The reader has to acknowledge that having health care problems, such as diabetes, heart disease, and smoking raises the risk of complications and adverse outcome. We are not all equal when it comes to our health and our potential for outcome. People that take good care of themselves should not be punished by being made to pay for defensive tactics that are necessary to cover the risks in the care of people who do not. Nor should they be responsible for those who have naturally occurring disease states that also raise the risk.

THE RISKS — AND RESERVES — WILL BE SHARED BY EVERYONE

The beauty of a universal health care system is that we will be bringing three hundred million people into the system and the risk will be

shared by everyone. Those with lower rankings will still pay something into the system even though the likelihood of a catastrophe is
very low. Even people with high risk will most often go through the
system without complication. That is why car-leasing companies still
lease cars to eighty-five-year-old people, because most of the time, the
car comes back intact and the risk is worth it. As soon as the number
of wrecked cars exceeds the money they make to lease them, there will
be fewer car rental companies willing to rent to eighty-five-year-old
drivers.

The same is true in medicine. Most of the time nothing adverse happens, but when it does, the liability costs are so high that we take steps
we should not need to take to protect against the alternative in the overall population. I would compare that to leasing the eighty-five-year-
old a car but paying a driver with a set of extra controls to drive with
them to keep them from having an accident. It would work, but the cost
would be exorbitant, just like it is with defensive medicine today.

The reserves that will accumulate will more than adequately cover
the risk of those people who are in a lower income bracket, keeping
their costs down. The government can contribute to that very small
proportion of people who are financially destitute, so their risk is also
covered.

Once the reserves are established, and the plan can evolve in several
cycles, we can get a feel for what the actual cost is in administering this
system. This system strives to give everyone a fighting chance. It is a
national system, and the overall cost of insuring three hundred million
people becomes affordable when the cost is shared by everyone. Then
the cost of the insurance can be reduced to meet the need. The fund
will be there for everyone's use only when it is needed, and no infernal
managed denial insurance company CEO can take the money out of
the fund as a bonus.

WHAT IF SOMEONE STILL WANTS TO SUE?

In this plan, nothing is mandatory as far as insuring oneself against
complications and adverse outcome. Patients are not mandated to purchase the insurance, but the overall cost would be so reasonable that
it would be unfathomable that anyone would reject it. Nonetheless,
there are hardheaded people in our country who would say that they
reserve the right to sue if something goes wrong in their treatment.
However, under the new system, it is likely that no doctor would elect
to treat such a patient — even in an emergency — without the insur-

ance against complication and adverse outcome in place.

In addition, the review boards that deal with problem cases are likely to rule the problem came from a complication or adverse outcome if the doctor stayed within the accepted standard of care. Furthermore, if the doctor were to be found to have acted within the written standard of care, it is unlikely that an attorney could be found willing to buck the system.

This would be foolhardy on the part of the patient, because with three hundred million people in the system, the cost of the insurance would be much less than the routine co-pays they have right now. It is a huge bargain for both sides. Lawyers could complain that this patient is being deprived of his rights, when in reality his rights are still present. No one can force any doctor to treat anyone, but unless the patient presents with something minor like a broken finger, no doctor is going to take the risk of taking a patient with Class IV co-morbidity in for treatment without risk protection. The doctor pays for his own liability for out-of-standard care and the patient pays a small fee to protect against complications and adverse outcome. Patients cannot have it both ways.

NEW LEGISLATION WILL BE NECESSARY TO PROTECT DOCTORS

Presently, across the nation there is a trend to close emergency rooms because the doctors have increased liability when taking care of emergency patients. With the appropriate protections built into the system, this trend could be reversed. This would have to take the shape of a "Good Samaritan" law for critically ill people. If the doctor takes the wrong kidney out of a critically ill person, the act would be a malpractice, but if a patient dies with an intestinal bleeding episode, who has stage II cancer, heart disease, kidney failure, and COPD, then some protection for the doctor needs to be built in. Without this protection, the system will break down and doctors are likely to choose defensive medicine and more conservative measures or worse, outright refusal to become involved.

Legislation will be needed to protect doctors against lawsuits that stem from caring for critically ill patients. Standards of care are frequently very complicated in these patients and they are likely to be injured or die just because of their condition. The public has to accept the fact that the physical condition of someone can have a devastating effect on any kind of health care. While most people respect this fact, there are large numbers of people who cannot accept the death of a loved one under any circumstances, and initiate legal action against doctors when they fail to stop death from occurring in a critically injured or ill patient, or simply a very aged patient whose time has come.

SUMMARY

In the 2008 Presidential election cycle, the major candidates stated that Americans must take control of their health, but urging people to do better on their own has been a huge failure in our country. There are going to be people who *do not* take care of themselves and do the things necessary to keep their health care problems to a minimum. Under my proposed plan, they will still demand health care — and they deserve it — but there will be conditions. This ranking system will provide appropriate protections for the patient, as well as the doctor and extend the standard of care with increased protection. The standards of care that control health care will be different depending upon the classification of the patient. The patient will get a more complicated treatment pattern with the obvious increased testing and procedures becoming necessary, as the complexity of the problem escalates in severity. What this system does do is eliminate the need for ordering of tests at a Class 4 level for a very simple procedure to try to protect against a lawsuit. We have a caricature of this operating right now. Anesthesia has taken to seeking "clearance" for patients with histories of a myriad of diseases. I have seen elderly patients with many different past problems ordered to have pre-surgical testing, including an entire raft of cardiac tests run for something as simple as a Carpal Tunnel Syndrome, or Trigger Finger Release, surgeries that barely take ten minutes to complete. This system will ultimately eliminate the need for defensive medicine and its inherent high cost. The patient with a higher rating could pay a slightly higher cost of insurance against complication and adverse outcome but not so much as to discourage treatment. The higher rating may have a standard of care that demands higher testing, but coordinating the procedure or treatment might obviate all the defensive tests ordered and lower the cost immensely.

In summary, the day of the doctor necessarily bearing the entire burden of the risk of complication and adverse outcome has to end if we want to have affordable, complete, universal care.

Chapter Twelve

STEP III
MEDICARE AND ENTITLEMENTS

I PLACED MEDICARE and entitlements in the third step of this three-step plan because they deserve special attention. This plan mandates that the government give up the Medicare/Medicaid entitlement plan that is scheduled to fail in the year 2016. This plan is based on the premise that this country demands universal health care for all citizens but not government-controlled universal health care. Every citizen in this country has the right to full and complete health care. Our seniors are not receiving this right now, and that needs to change. Bringing the senior citizens and all people on Medicare and Medicaid into the fold will allow the costs to be spread across the entire population. That will reduce the costs for us all.

In my lifetime, I have seen Medicare metamorphose from a good idea to a disappointment to a tragedy. Presently, Medicare cannot pay for health care, at least as most doctors define it.

Right up front, I want to state that the problems inherent in the Medicare/Medicaid programs are not the fault of the people running the system or working within the system. They have been given an impossible task by the government — to try to treat patients without adequate funds to do so. How Medicare workers have done what they have until now leaves me in sheer wonderment. Nonetheless, as the Baby Boomer generation nears the time when they will enter the program, the numbers are simply no longer in our favor.

As it has passed through history, the Baby Boomer generation has had a huge effect on society. At first, the maternity wards were overwhelmed with an abundance of births. People wanted to have their babies in a hospital, so hospitals had to expand their obstetric departments. Then, as the children grew, we needed more elementary schools, high schools, colleges and universities. We needed more hospital beds, more books, more entertainment, more insurance plans, more government programs, more cars, more highways, more housing, more everything. Now, the Baby Boomers are about to enter the Medicare program just at the time when its future is becoming increasingly unclear. It does not take a college degree to understand the math.

The SGR (Sustainable Growth Rate) formula, or any other formula that can be designed, will fail without a massive influx of more money. With the economy teetering on collapse, money would have to be borrowed each year to prop up the program, and that is simply not necessary or possible. The program was mal-designed in the beginning, and just putting a fresh coat of paint on a program that has moved consistently toward failure over the years is not going to work any longer. Furthermore, America cannot continue to strangle her doctors without the system's ultimate failure, causing a disaster.

The purpose of this book has been to introduce changes in the way we do things in health care so that the entire population can share in the wonderful things we have achieved. With the entirety of that in mind, let us explore a way to move through the new millennium with a program that will take the worry away from our senior citizens forever.

THE WAY TO SOLVE THE DILEMMA OF MEDICARE/MEDICAID IS TO *ELIMINATE* IT

The Medicare and Medicaid programs are, without a doubt one of the biggest problems we have in this country's health care. (Hereafter, for the ease of discussion, let the term "Medicare" represent both the Medicare and Medicaid programs.) We all know about the impending failure. The latest predictions are coming in with the revelation that a large segment of the Baby Boomer generation has joined Medicare through Social Security Disability because of obesity, heart disease, lung disease, arthritis, and of all things, depression. Medicare was not counting on this group of people entering the system in large numbers for up to ten more years. (One blog recently estimated that Medicare could fail as soon as 2011.)

As we have seen before, insurance of any kind is defined as a fund, which we all put our money into and remove it only when we need to utilize it. With Medicare, just as it is in the private side, someone else is taking the money out of the program. In this case, the money is removed to enforce the mountain of regulations that accompanies the entitlement program. Unfortunately, now many people who have paid into the system for their entire adult lives are facing the fact that they may not receive appropriate and complete care for what they have paid.

The money spent on Medicare is supposed to be used for nothing but health care. However, like all government entitlement programs, as time goes on, the program becomes top heavy with bureaucratic functions, and the thrust of the fund becomes supporting the bureaucracy rather than providing service to the people for whom it was intended.

The money is placed in the hands of well-meaning people, but the burdens of bureaucracy actually force them to be financially irresponsible, so that a lot of the money goes toward things that are not health care. The figures for enforcing the regulations are cleverly hidden from the public but this author has heard several high-ranking government officials and speakers at medical conventions estimate the cost at $400 billion per year. That seems unrealistic to me. No matter what the figure actually is, I am sure the public will never know the true amount.

The programs are much too large to adequately police and keep on track. Abuses multiply as clever people find ways to get the money out of the government illegally or unnecessarily. The government's response to this is to enact piles of regulations, and before too much time passes, the fund may spend more money on policing itself than providing service.

THE TRAGEDY OF MEDICARE

Medicare has become a tragedy. The best thing that could happen to this country is to disband it and create another program that is oriented toward the people whom it is intended to serve. It would be a heroic effort if the government would itself take this bold step, but the likelihood of this happening is microscopic. Once those mega-giant programs are created, they become like cancers, consuming everything in their way and destroying the host. In this particular situation, the host is the American public and their need is health care, not bureaucracy. America is the most innovative country ever to grace the earth, but she is also very wasteful and irresponsible with her money. America can do better. She just needs to be shown the way.

Ever since the Medicare program was started, it has been in trouble. It began as part of the "Great Society" of Lyndon Baines Johnson in 1964. The concept was honorable, and the intent of the program was, on the surface, to provide health care. It started out as an assist to American seniors to help them pay their medical bills, but under the lobbying pressure from the AMA, the program was expanded to approach full and complete health care.

America would have been better off if the government had just collected enough tax money to purchase a standard health care insurance plan for each of its elderly citizens. As it stands now, Medicare has come full circle, and at best can be called an assist to help seniors pay their medical bills. The difference now is that in the 1960s and early 1970s, it cost a total of $356 per year per person, so the assist was a considerable help. Recently, The National Coalition of Health care reported that total health care spending in the US reached $2.4 trillion in 2007 resulting in costs of $8000 per person per year in equivalent dollars, and the "assist" that our seniors are getting is embarrassing and un-American.

Medicare was poorly conceived, but instead of just revamping the program and starting over, the government has just added more and more regulations. Many of the regulations conflict with each other. Just a very few years after Medicare was created, Richard Nixon declared a massive health care emergency and predicted a failure if the problem, which was estimated at $60 billion, was not managed. This came at a time when the total cost of health care was $356 per person per year for a total of $70 billion. Medicare had run up a debt of $60 billion on its own. The government paid the bill by ultimately breaking into the Social Security Trust Fund. That break in the faith with the American people should have been a red flag, but the country was consumed with the Vietnam War and the theft went virtually unnoticed. The government responded to the inability to pay for the service by making a hundred new changes in the Social Security Act that cut fees and enacted other regulations.

The program then underwent a series of changes that paid less for a service than the service was worth with the result that, instead of just dropping off the enrollment, doctors and hospitals began to shift costs to the insurance companies, making them pay much more than their share. People on all sides of the fray were too hardheaded to admit that there was a problem and the entire system of American health care began to degenerate into the tragedy it has become today.

In both the public and private sector, America, the economic giant has fallen to the bottom of the ranks of industrialized nations by having the worst health care system of the lot. As its ability to foot the bills failed, the government became a huge bully. It forced insulting rates of pay for services on providers.

THE RISE OF FRAUD AND ABUSE, AND THE GOVERNMENT'S RESPONSE

As the government paid less, providers just simply found other ways to get the "easy government money" by overuse of the system, and intentional fraud and abuse. Once there was "free" government health care, some patients abused the system with overuse, and no control was created to manage that problem. Providers kept up their income by cost shifting their government losses to the private insurance companies. Other types of abuse of the system began to occur as the regulations that were heaped on the pile began to conflict with one another. Providers did not know which regulation to follow. The huge maze of regulations choked the system. The answer by the government was to pass bill after bill and make new regulation upon new regulation, with the intent of controlling the mega-giant of chaos.

The Medicare and Medicaid Fraud and Abuse Amendments of 1977 further tightened the noose. The HCFA (Heath Care Financing Act) was one of the programs in "The Medicare and Medicaid Fraud and Abuse Amendments" of 1977. The HCFA was initiated to manage Medicare and Medicaid programs. The OIG (Office of the Inspector General) became the enforcement arm of HCFA. Instead of just kicking the cheaters out of the system, however, they punished everyone, and the bureaucracy grew for the purpose of retribution.

"The Deficit Reduction Act" of 1983 included the new term, "DRG," for "Diagnostically Related Groups." It was a way to bundle groups of costs into one bill that traditionally were paid individually, and it really began to strangle hospitals and doctors. If, for instance, you have a broken hip, you fall under the DRG for a hip fracture and no matter how much money is spent by the hospital taking care of you; they get a single pre-determined fee that generally cannot be modified. This is where hospitals lose a ton of money. Hospitals also shifted costs to the private insurance companies.

Hospitals responded by shortening patients' length of stay and Medicare responded by reducing the payment for the DRG when they realized hospitals were safely able to shorten stays.

These acts were all followed by the 1985 "Balanced Budget and Emergency Deficit Control Act" and the "Gramm-Rudman-Hollings Act" that allowed the President to cut fees if he so desired. This was followed by years of "Omnibus Budget Reconciliation Acts," as the government sought to cut its losses. It has never worked.

Finally, managed denial was entered into the formula, and now doctors are nearly being run out of business, as the managed denial companies seek to pay doctors and other providers' bottom-of-the-barrel fees. The government has contracted with managed denial companies to take over the part B costs (doctors, physical therapy, outpatient services), and now they are instituting the same strangling policies that they are on the private side. It has become ipso facto health care rationing. They cut and they cut and they cut services but the providers are left with the liability for shoddy health care forced upon them by the mountain of regulations that has accumulated.

The federal government has clearly been a huge player in the destruction of our health care system. Simply put, one cannot pay less than the cost of something for very long before the quality is wrenched out of the system or it simply fails.

A formula, called the SGR (Sustainable Growth Rate), was then designed to try to resuscitate the struggling program. This formula reduced payments to providers based on the number of people in the program. With higher numbers of entitlements beneficiaries, reimbursements were diminished, despite the fact that they were already lower than it cost the provider to care for patients. As the years passed, it became clear the system was going to implode.

MEDICARE HAS BECOME A HUGE POLITICAL FOOTBALL

When one politician talks bravely and honestly about trying to fix the problem, the other side competing for public office starts shouting, "the other guy is going to take away your Medicare!" to scare the public. Elections teetered as the elderly with their huge voting bloc were put in the middle of a huge political tug-of-war.

At the age of seventy, just about all that anyone has left is their health care, and even bad health care is better than no health care. As soon as anyone broaches the subject, however, the competition will hammer them with lies that Medicare will be taken away. Political types have become petrified to attempt to get the public to go along with the changes needed to make the system work, so we just languish in the political sewage that Medicare has been forced to live in.

Most recently, in July of 2008, Congress sought to enforce the law that was passed in 2005 that mandated physicians' fees were to be cut 40 % by 2010. That single desperate act by the irresponsible Congress would have put many doctors out of business or caused them to discontinue services to senior citizens. The President of the American College of Family Physicians published the fact that if those cuts were to go into effect, the majority of family doctors would be forced to drop off the Medicare program and either go out of business or seriously downsize their practice. Seniors and doctors alike deluged their Representatives and Senators with complaints and threats.

Congress passed the cuts and then went home to see what would happen over the July 4, 2008 holiday but they soon realized they had to do something and quickly. Congress responded by passing a bill that reinstituted fees back to their previous level from the 10.6% cut that was allowed to go on the books July 1, 2008. President Bush vetoed the bill because managed denial insurance companies would not collect the fees that he had guaranteed them, but Congress quickly overrode his veto.

This scenario clearly illustrates the dire straits that Medicare has fallen into. In his recent dealings with the economic stimulus, President Obama has said that health care in the future will be financed "by raising taxes on the rich and cutting payments to providers, hospitals and doctors." Mr. Obama was one of the Senators that voted to replace the lost doctor fees by repealing the 10.6% cut in physician fees in July 2008. Eight months later, he is now calling for reducing payments to doctors at a time when 54% of all doctors have said they will likely quit in the next two years, naming low pay as one of the foremost reasons. This seesawing public policy clearly indicates that none of our elected officials has the foggiest idea about what is wrong with medicine in America.

Mr. Obama promised "change we can live with," but neither physician nor patient can survive with the changes he has come up with. Forget the problem with the economy. If health care crashes — and it appears to be heading in that direction — we will not *have* an economy. If President Obama thinks he can save Medicare by further cutting physician and hospital pay, Medicare will fail during his first term for lack of a physician force.

CHANGE IS NEEDED

Well, *I*, for one, am not afraid to scream, *change!* I am not afraid to state the obvious and try to help my President understand what changes are really needed. What is going on in the health care of our senior citizens is already a disgrace. It must be changed because it *has* failed; seniors will soon be without even skeleton health care, and we are likely to witness a mass exodus of doctors out of the system.

We change our government frequently, but the people who keep being elected do nothing to contain the growing problem government health care has become. We must act and it must be soon. We must avoid the mistakes of the past and not create an even larger government ogre to replace the disaster we presently have. Eventually, the government will have to cut its losses and take a different path.

I want the reader to understand why the system is failing, and how the system I am promoting will solve the problem. The trick will be to get the American public to understand the program and to accept it. Unfortunately, it may then be just as difficult to get the American government to make the change.

That is why Medicare has been relegated to Step III in the three-step process. We first have to make the system work for everyone not enrolled in an entitlement system. When the public witnesses the cost savings and the overall controlled atmosphere, the government can just simply use tax dollars they already collect to purchase the necessary premiums for everyone on entitlements. There will no longer be a need for the expensive enforcement actions. The program is *self-governing, self-evolving, self-policing and self-correcting* all through *written standards of care*. In short, we will make the US government an offer they cannot refuse.

WHAT'S WRONG WITH MEDICARE?

Before we delve into the dark abyss of a bad program, let us set a few ground rules. If I try to explain everything that I feel is wrong with the Medicare program, this book would make *War and Peace* look like a term paper. In fact, there is so much wrong with Medicare as it relates to the general care of a sick person that this book would turn into a never-ending story. Here, I intend to make only a few points as to how badly the system has failed and why we should replace it with a new plan.

FROM THE BEGINNING, MEDICARE COULD NOT AFFORD TO BE IN HEALTH CARE

The first concept is that, from the beginning, Medicare could not afford to be in health care. There were no rigid standards of care, which controlled a doctor's care of the sick and injured. It was designed as an open-ended system, allowing doctors to practice their "art" as they saw fit. The designers of Medicare were shortsighted, as they thought it could pay for everything.

As with any business in America, people tried to get the best money for their efforts. Some businesses are happy with a reasonable return on their money, but others are not content unless they get a king's ransom for minimal effort. In this respect, government programs are always poorly designed — there are always loopholes in the code, and some people search out those loopholes to pay less or receive more. Just look at the US tax system as an example. Medicare was no different. Very few doctors, hospitals, and allied health providers, as well as makers of medical equipment searched for the loopholes and used them for unethical purposes, and in some instances, defrauded the government out of millions. Unfortunately, as the government does frequently, Medicare interpreted that as meaning all providers were dishonest and sought regulations that were overkill. After a few egregious financial attacks on the system, the regulations began to mount up. There were no agreed-upon standards to conduct affairs by. If Medicare had been able to enact the standards this plan proposes, there would have been no need to lose trillions of dollars in enforcement efforts.

THE FRAUD AND ABUSE WERE COSTLY TO FIGHT

The government had to prosecute violators, but relatively few were ever caught. I remember one lecture in medical school about the government programs that could have been mistaken for a "how-to" course on how to game the system. The amount of money that has been spent to investigate the fraud and abuse, and try to stop it is out of proportion to the amount recovered.

It is difficult to track the funds spent on enforcement. Statistics from the FBI indicate that they are charged with investigating a portion of the health care fraud. This is not necessarily Medicare fraud; plenty of health care fraud in the country has nothing to do with Medicare. The country now has more than a $2.4 trillion total medical budget, which represents 17% of the GDP. There is an estimated 3 to 10% rate of fraud to the tune of $65 billion that we know of. The Congress funds the FBI with $114 million each year for health care fraud. Using that sum to investigate and recover lost funds, they are successful in retrieving only $1.6 billion per year out of the known $65 billion in fraud. It is difficult to tell how much of the FBI efforts are devoted to fighting fraud in the Medicare system but the efforts of enforcement are way under-funded in the amount of money provided compared to the success of catching the fraudulent providers. But it is only FBI money.

Responsibility for the fraud and abuse is shared by HHS (Health and Human Services), the OIG, the FBI and probably others. As stated above, the funds spent on enforcing the Medicare rules and seeking out fraud and abuse are difficult to track, but I have heard the figure of $400 billion per year as a benchmark figure for the enforcement of regulations and administration of the program. It has been reported that if Medicare regulations were to be stacked one on top of the other, the pile would be taller than a two-story building. Somehow, this makes the figure of $400 billion per year to try to enforce the regulations seem believable.

According to figures provided by the CMS (Center for Medicare Services), the government office that controls all Medicare and Medicaid services, that figure exceeds what we spend for our seniors' health care. Four hundred billion dollars a year would go a long way towards solving the problem seniors have of paying for their prescription medications.

The reader is cautioned not to allow this speculation to be taken to heart — there is no way to find out exactly how much is being spent to enforce regulations and administer the plan — but the concept here is that it really makes no difference. If the government has to spend even $1 to enforce rules, then the program is set up incorrectly and it is already a failure. While there will always be people who try to take advantage of the system, expending health care dollars to try to go backward to find them has already been proven a failure. Any health care plan worth the effort will already have controls built in to head this off. This failure has always been the major flaw in Medicare, and any entitlement program for that matter. Once the program goes off target to try to put out the fires of fraud and abuse, then the battle has already been lost. If the reader cannot comprehend this simple fact, then socialized medicine is in your future and your health care will be spent in administration costs, retroactive auditing, and all the government knee-jerk waste that characterizes Medicare today. Beware. There is a much better way to handle your health care. You, as a citizen need to realize this and be ready to force the change so that your health care dollars go toward and only go toward your health care needs, and not to support some giant bureaucracy.

This new plan would eliminate the need for the government to spend anything in recovery efforts to keep doctors, hospitals, and ancillary health services in line.

What we are witnessing is the agonal rhythm of the heartbeat of

Medicare and Medicaid in America ["agonal" "of, pertaining to or symptomatic of agony, esp. paroxysmal distress, as the death throes"]. Where the end will come is when the Baby Boomer generation becomes fully vested in Medicare entitlement. There are so many of them that even the simple unintentional fraud and abuse that occurs will be even more difficult to track, and there simply will not be enough money to perform routine retrospective investigations and still pay for health care. No matter what tricks the government will try to prop it up, the old dinosaur will just topple over from the inability to support its own weight and cost. Trying to resuscitate the program with a defibrillator-type influx of new borrowed money is simply foolhardy when there are better ways to handle their health care.

This is not France. This is not Italy. This is not Great Britain. What works for the relatively small populations in those countries will not work in the US. Trying to initiate a SPEC type "one size fits all" medical care program in America will be all consuming, and the majority of the funds will end up in the hands of people doing things other than health care.

Once again, health care is not an envelope with "health care" written on the outside, but a fund that you draw on only when you are sick or injured. No one else, including the government, needs to have their greedy little hands in your health care fund.

ENDLESS MEDICARE RULES AND REGULATIONS

The large list of Medicare regulations is overpowering. There are so many rules that are so confusing that an individual practitioner cannot possibly know them all or possibly comply with all of them. In this way, Medicare and their investigators can walk into any practitioner's office, hospital or business and hand out fines, interest and penalties. Sadly, this is the boon of the program. They only have to show congressional oversight committees that they are policing the program, when in reality they are still missing overwhelming amounts of accidental fraud and abuse, not to mention purposeful fraud and abuse that are not even related to doctors' care.

The rules change every year and the individual practitioners are required to know the changes. In order to know and understand the rule changes, one must know the system to begin with, but it is too large for an individual physician to understand, much less keep up with the rules. Doctors are so overwhelmed with patient care that it would almost take a separate education equal to that of medical or law school just to begin to understand the system. They simply do not have the time to do both. That opens up the door to unintentional violations of the rules.

THE FRAUD AND ABUSE RULES

In order for the reader to understand the fraud and abuse rules, I will attempt a simple explanation: "fraud" is an *intentional* breach of the rules, and "abuse" is an *unintentional* breach of the rules.

For instance, if a doctor reads the newspaper and sees that his patient died in a house fire, and sends in an additional three office visits after the patient dies, clearly that is fraud, but there is virtually no way Medicare will know the exact date of death unless it specifically investigates that particular patient. Three office visits is unlikely to be noticed by the system, so the cheating doctor can receive an additional three fees that are not legitimate. That is true fraud. It is an intentional attempt to defraud the system for financial gain.

Abuse in the form of unintentional type of fraud occurs in the form of an accidental or unintentional procurement of government funds. The problem becomes complicated because if the doctor does not understand the payment system and he repeatedly bills in a similar fashion for the service every time, he creates a record of abuse that is then deemed intentional by the government. In short, if the unintentional *abuse* is repetitive, then it becomes *fraud*. Therein lays the trapdoor for the physician. The word "fraud" is a like a light switch for the public — that is all they have to hear since the public already has the impression that doctors are filthy rich, and to say a doctor is committing "fraud" makes everyone mad. That makes it easy for Medicare audits to implicate doctors without public outcry.

As we will see, the government does not set a fee for which a doctor is paid for utilizing his training and experience. If, for example, I were to be paid a standard fee for a visit for a sore shoulder, there would be no fraud and abuse unless I just falsified the record. Instead, they create a complicated formula by which I must replicate the entire history and physical of the medical record of this patient to prove I actually did something. Most doctors cannot understand the complicated formula and get themselves into trouble with fraud and abuse because the system is entirely unlike anything they are used to.

With each passing year, Medicare edits their payment schemes with things called "Correct Coding Initiatives" (CCI edits) to continue to reduce what they will pay for. The codes change all the time. As the money noose tightens, Medicare bundles treatments together to try to save money. For instance, in my line of work, during one surgery, I perform three procedures that if done separately would get a separate charge. Each one bears a liability if something goes wrong with it. Medicare bundles them all into the charge for the one surgery and I lose the charges for the other two. There exists a ninety-day "global period" and if something happens within the global period to the patient then I am not paid for any further treatment. In addition, any supplies that I must use, such as dressings, bandages, casts, and the like, all come out of my pocket. If I cannot afford the bandages and the patient gets an infection, then I have a liability issue to deal with, including the fact that I will not be paid to take care of the infection. Therefore, the rule is I lose money on every Medicare patient I treat.

The trick with the CCI edits lies in the fact that the CMS continually bundles charges into larger and larger bundles. The doctor has to employ people who specifically watch the CCI edits all the time. If the employee unknowingly bills for a bundled treatment or procedure that was just combined with another that was previously allowed, then it is denied. The continuing changes are nearly impossible to keep up with for a small business office.

Retroactive audits are the most expensive way to try to control fraud. If rigid standards of care were in charge of the process, it would be easier to control. It would be so much easier to stop the fox at the henhouse door rather than deal with the disaster of catching the fox in the henhouse after the damage is done.

Some of the rules in place are just absurd. For example, a doctor can be fined for not signing every piece of paper in the chart, even though the doctor is the only one to use the charts, and is the only one responsible for creating the record in the first place. Medicare auditors can even walk into an office, start picking up charts, and hold them by the chart covers, and every piece of loose paper that falls out can generate a substantial fine. I have heard the number $2000 for every piece of paper they can shake out of the chart. The rules are so complex and so overwhelming to the individual doctor that Medicare could virtually walk into any doctor's office, audit the records, and find *some kind* of violation.

Even more discouraging is the fact of how often the system changes. My office manager informs me that every day when she checks her e-mail, many notices come out from CMS. Daily, there are e-mails present that she has to click on to read. They are not just one or two line notices; they are entire articles about how the change relates to myriads of other changes that were involved with myriads of previous changes. She used to print them out and give them to the office staff, but if my office staff took the time to read all the changes, they would have no time to get anything else done. There is no way, and *I mean no way* that anyone could possibly keep up with all of this.

A doctor spends almost all of his time trying to take care of sick people. There is no time in the day to try to comply with this mega-giant of confusion. I took a mock survey in the doctors' lounge recently and not one doctor even knew of the Medicare changes nor had they read them. Recently, the US Congress passed the largest spending bill in the history of this country. It was reported that not one elected official had even read the bill. The difference between them and medical providers is Congressmen do not have to face audits that charge them with fraud, even though that one act was the largest act of fraud in the history of the world.

Not only is the CMS bundling everything a doctor does together, they are cutting the fees paid for doing so. Just two years ago, the head of the CMS made the bold statement that "the cuts in reimbursement will continue until we see sufficiently larger numbers of doctors who drop off the program." Well, if the National Physicians Foundation Survey means anything, America is headed for a big fall. Once the CMS reaches their goal of doctors who have left the system, simply raising fees to the remaining doctors will not help — there will not be enough doctors to take care of all the patients.

Until now, doctors have been afraid to drop out of the program because of the experience in Massachusetts several years ago, where, as soon as doctors began to leave the program, legislators wrote laws mandating doctors to take care of Medicare and Medicaid patients or they would not keep their state licenses. Now we truly are reaching the state of an oligarchy.

So every year, the doctor's electric and heating bill goes up, their taxes go up, the price of gasoline goes up, their malpractice insurance fees go up — everything goes up except the doctor's reimbursement. In addition, insurance companies now base their payments on what Medicare pays. Many practices have failed because of inadequate reimbursements for their services and many, many more are sure to follow.

Evaluation and Management visits to the doctor's office

Let us explore another type of cut and rulemaking that is resulting in doctors failing. This has to do with the program for "E & M" visits to the doctor's office.

The government has a saying that they go by in their quest to ferret out fraud and abuse: *"If it is not documented, it is not done. If it is not documented, then it is fraud or abuse to be paid for it. It is ill-gotten gain."*

When I first graduated from medical school, I was taught skills of evaluation of a patient. I am not referring to the more complex examination of a patient, just the inspection of a patient as they walked into my examining room and upon first glance. With that first look, I can tell things about the color of the patient's skin; if they have a full complement of blood or if they are anemic; if are they intoxicated; if they have arthritis; if they are alert, oriented and cooperative; if they have painful movements; if they have all their appendages, if they have an odor; if they smoke; if they are laboring to breathe; if they have stains on their pants where they leak urine; if they are unclean; and so on. Your visit to the doctor is an exercise in all the five senses, and most patients are unaware of the surveillance of the body and mind.

Doctors can list traits, signs, and symptoms that patients do not even think are being noticed. That is what we are trained to do. All doctors do this and, as in any profession, some are better than others are. Before the interview is complete, most doctors have a good idea about the general condition of the patient. However, under the present system, a doctor gets no credit for his expertise. He must document everything he sees or it is fraud to be paid for. Medicare has, thus denigrated the expertise our doctors have spent long years acquiring. They are hamstringing the world's greatest physicians in the name of "Big Brother" control.

In the quest to try to make ends meet, some smart government type realized money could be saved if they simply made it more difficult for a doctor to do his job. By complicating the workload and tying reimbursement to it, they could limit the number of patients a doctor could see, thereby reducing the amount of dollars going to each doctor's office, and in the end, reclaim monies paid out when the doctor trips over the regulations. This is a type of health care rationing that serves no good purpose, but it is one way they can make their SGR (Sustainable Growth Rate) formula seem successful. They perfected their plan by instituting E&M rules for a doctor to see a patient in the office.

QUANTITY VS. QUALITY

Before we delve into this, remember that it used to be that a patient went to the doctor and there was a set office fee for the visit. Not so now. In my own office, I had a two-tiered system. If I had a relatively simple visit, I charged one fee. If the problem was more complex, I had a larger fee. It was simple to use, it worked out well, and no one was charged for something in excess or less than the service was worth. The E & M plan that Medicare forced on me, on the other hand, is so complex that I simply cannot understand what Medicare feels is an appropriate fee for my care. The formula to try to calculate the fees is so confusing and so time-consuming that my staff cannot keep up with it.

Under this system, there are five levels of visit, each with its own level of payment. Each level has a complicated formula for things that have to be documented to be paid. As the patient enters the office, rather than "evaluating and managing" the condition of his patient, the doctor is already forced into thinking about what he has to do to be paid a reasonable fee. The doctor is forced to begin to calculate the *quantity* of pieces of evidence he collects rather than the *quality* of the information he evaluates. This intervention into the sacred relationship of a doctor and his patient forces the doctor to violate his sacred Hippocratic Oath each time he sees a patient.

Twenty years ago, the government did this to the nursing profession, and as a result, the bulk of their job has become charting rather than caring for sick people.

This intrusion on the needs of the sick and injured by the government is revolting. The government is forcing doctors to be more concerned with what is on the paper than with what lies within the being of their patient. This one factor, more than any other, is the reason why government has to be taken out of health care and forever kept out of health care.

THEN AND NOW

Before the E & M rule changes, I had a little pocket tape recorder that I used to dictate my notes. If any of these traits were outstanding, I would include it in my dictation. All else was superfluous. It was unnecessary and it cluttered the medical record. These things were not documented because they were unnecessary to do my job as a subspecialist.

Things that were important were documented. Things that were not important were not documented. It was as simple as that. The record was concise and uncluttered. Now, however, Medicare requires that I mention something about at least ten organ systems or I am paid at a Level 2 or 3. Most of that is unnecessary for a doctor's record unless it is the primary care doctor. Only pertinent changes from the original history and physical exam need be documented. However, because of the lack of a central digital database, every time a patient comes into an office, the same information has to be *re*-documented. If it is not documented, I could face huge fines, penalties, and interest in an audit if a standard fee is charged. In this way, the government ties up my time with busy work so that I cannot see as many patients. This is health care rationing by the simplest means: just make the doctor so busy he cannot see as many patients, and then overwhelm his billing personnel with a system so complicated that the chance of an error is always in the favor of the CMS, allowing them to force the doctor to repay his fee with penalties and interest.

Since we went to the new system, as with many other doctors I have talked to, my billings are down significantly, an indication the corrupt system works. Insurance companies have taken up the same program and physicians like me are struggling to stay in business. I used to be paid a fee for my knowledge and my competence as a physician and surgeon but now the government is forcing me to be a record keeper.

YET MORE RULES

Well, even if you document everything you do, Medicare does not want to pay these fees. ("Not documented, not done, not paid.") After the new documentation rules were put into place, every doctor had to document an entirely new history and physical in order to be paid even a less-than-respectable fee. We have already learned what repetitive medicine has done to the system. This repetition would be eliminated under the new system.

On top of that, the doctor had mandatory time limits piled on top of everything else. These were based on what level of bill he was charging. For instance, for a Level 3 visit, which pays less than what it costs to get a tire changed, the doctor has to have at least thirty minutes of *face-to-face time* with a patient.

Most everyone knows that doctors are inundated with patients. There is no way all the health care being done could be done if the doctor had to spend thirty minutes in front of a patient just to get what an uneducated tire jockey gets paid to change a tire in five minutes. That rule means that in an eight-hour day, the doctor could see just sixteen patients and make little more than what a tire jockey gets paid. The kicker is that the tire jockey does not have to spend fifteen years in school to learn a very difficult profession and he is unlikely to be sued if something goes awry.

An E & M visit has five levels of payment. Levels 4 and 5 are the visits that pay the most, and so the rules require more points of examination, history, and medical decision-making be present on the history and physical record. Those things are easy enough to do, but it does take extended time to do so. The sad result is that a patient's history has already been recorded many places and times when it could be in a digital document that the doctor could download (See Chapter Eight).

As we have seen, this repetition and replication of treatment costs an immense amount of money, and it is fraught with holes in information, as patients frequently forget pieces of their history, no matter what their age. By requiring doctors to replicate this information over and over again, the cost actually goes up, not down.

Finally, the process of slowing the doctor down also cuts down on the experience of a doctor. Doctors gain experience that they draw from by seeing many different conditions, and seeing the results of their diagnosis and treatment. The more patients they see, the more experience they gain, the better doctors they are. Hogtying our medical professionals in this way contributes to doctors' inexperience and adds to the potential for the very medical mistakes the government is howling about.

MEDICAL DECISION-MAKING

At the end, Medicare threw in a section on medical decision making, which has to do with how much effort has to be put into making the diagnosis. So what does the doctor do to increase the amount of his medical decision making to qualify for a higher level of reimbursement? Well, an X-ray could help. I could ask for the patient's old records from his family doctor to be brought to the office. If the patient has a family member present, I could ask some questions of the family member. Then I could list a huge differential diagnosis.

Several things qualify as medical decision making, including X-rays, surgical treatment, physical therapy, splints, casts, injections, and prescriptions. If someone comes in just for a routine History and Physical Examination, and nothing is really wrong, the medical decision-making is near zero, which means the doctor gets paid at the lowest level of payment, 1 or 2, even if he has to take thirty to sixty minutes to come to that conclusion. If the doctor has to take some action on the patient's behalf, then he can raise his level of payment to one of the higher levels by providing some of the above listed things. For instance, if a doctor gives a prescription, the rate of pay could go up to Level 4 if everything else in the History and Physical Examination reaches comprehensive status.

Medicare does not have to agree with the doctor's idea of medical necessity, however, as the following will illustrate.

AN EXAMPLE

The really sad thing here is that a doctor like me could be cited in an audit for acting in either of two ways. If my patient came in to see me for a clicking finger, which is what we call a "trigger finger," I am put into the situation of initially trying to decide how much effort I have to put into the E & M visit. The government can fine me for putting in too much effort to make the diagnosis. In their mind, they could say that it was medically unnecessary for me to do a comprehensive history and physical when the patient suffers only from a single trigger [or "click-ing"] finger.

Well, what if the patient is actually suffering from rheumatoid arthritis and the trigger finger is just the presenting symptom? Once, I was led to the diagnosis of AIDS by a swollen clicking finger. The entire physical finding was so out of proportion that I thought I would order some laboratory work. It came back HIV positive with a virus load so high that it made the diagnosis AIDS. When I told him he was HIV positive, he pulled up his T-shirt and asked me to look at something on his back. There was a Kaposi Sarcoma (the hallmark cancer typical of people with AIDS) that was as large as a golf ball. He told me his family doctor had been giving him cortisone cream to rub on it for two years. Therefore, if I had elected to just treat the finger and do a point-specific examination, then I risked a medical malpractice suit for failure to diagnose the condition of AIDS if the patient had come down with serious complications, or died.

MEDICINE CANNOT BE PRACTICED IN THIS WAY

A doctor has to have a set way of going about his profession without trying to figure out which mode of treatment is the least likely to get into trouble with an audit.

On the other hand, if I take the time to delve into the patient's history and physical and do not find something like rheumatoid arthritis or AIDS and only find a simple trigger finger, then the government can fine me for performing service that is in excess of the medical necessity. When I asked about this in a Medicare update seminar, a Medicare representative responded by saying, "What are you complaining about, doctor? It's only your time?"

Most of the time, I have no idea what to do with the regulations and I am sure most of my colleagues feel the same. So a doctor can be fined for "up coding" that the auditor feels is too much, or "down coding" like many doctors do to try to avoid an audit, or for simply putting too much effort into the task.

Is it any wonder why 54% of America's doctors have indicated they are going to quit? We cannot practice with this kind of micromanaging hovering over us. I, like many of my colleagues, have become so fed up with the process that I no longer enjoy taking care of patients. And the scariest thing is that we could be fined out of existence, or even put in jail, depending on how our practice is envisioned or judged by an auditor, without ever getting a chance to defend ourselves at a trial on the issue.

Please notice there is no standard of care that indicates or mandates the choices for treatment. The government pays no heed to the "generally accepted standards of care" that we heard about earlier. Only the documentation counts. If desired, the same patient could be returned for several visits. By indicating the medical necessity of each visit, and increasing the level of invasive treatment each time, the visit could still qualify for a Level 4 E & M visit each time. In other words, if the chart is properly documented, the doctor could get away with "legalized fraud."

For most, if not all physicians, this is a plan for utter survival. Many doctors have had to opt for this method of treatment because they are not being paid enough to keep an office going. An auditor could, however, disagree with the medical necessity of his actions and levy a punishment on the doctor, and the doctor could say nothing about it. He is guilty until he exhausts never-ending hearings that could bankrupt him.

The reader can easily see that Medicare has so complicated the process with such intense documentation and rules that it has ruined the process of a simple doctor's visit and, in turn, they design the regulations and procedures in a way to fine the doctor for whatever he chooses to do. I feel like the soldier on the Vietnam battlefield who had to run over six hundred yards of open ground to get ammunition while the enemy opened fire on him.

THE CASE OF THE FAMILY DOCTOR

Let us see how this works in the case of the typical family doctor. The same E & M rules exist for the family doctor as others, but he does not necessarily have the increasingly more advanced and expensive treatments for someone, for instance, as a surgeon would. All the doctor needs to do is to perform a complex E & M visit the first time around, continue to write prescriptions to be paid at the higher levels, and to make the necessary documentation entries in the chart. The fact is that Medicare pays family doctors so little that they are forced into these practices or die on the vine.

The visits can be programmed so that a prescription is *always* due. I hate even to think of this, but is it any wonder why one sees senior citizens walking around with a garbage-bag-full of prescription bottles?

I was taught in medical school that if a patient comes in with more than five medications on his list, then the prescribing doctor has no idea what he is doing. Unfortunately, out of a literal need to survive, he may be *fully aware* of what he is doing. Things have changed in thirty years. We have better drugs for more conditions. Doctors are under constant pressure to treat everything patients want. Add to that the constant pressure of liability he has for *not* prescribing something and having to sit through a trial when something goes wrong. The premise is that it is generally better to *over-prescribe* to ease the liability problem. Patients have to pay for that because there are no standards of practice governing the conduct of the doctor that will provide him with the appropriate protection from a lawsuit.

If the doctor were paid an appropriate fee for what is done and if the standard of care controlled the treatment from the beginning, these problems would most assuredly go away. Without written standards and with the piling on of regulations and enforcements, however, Medicare has ended up being a tragedy of uncalculated proportion. The Step III program would solve all of these issues *and* cut the cost.

HOSPITAL DOCTORS HAVE TO BE COACHED ON HOW TO GAME THE SYSTEM

As Medicare and insurance companies strangle more and more doctors, and cause more of them to give up their private practices and quit or become hospital employees, the problem becomes worse. In order for visits to qualify as Level 4 E & M visits, the doctor can see only twelve patients a day because there is a forty-five-minute time requirement. That does not make the hospital administrator/employer very happy. Periodically, the employee doctor has to have a productivity review. The doctor sits in front of a supervisor and is shown a series of graphs comparing the productivity of the other staff members with his/her own. If the doctor does not keep up with everyone else, then the threat of being fired hangs heavy in the air. In order for the doctor to see twelve patients a day and still stay productive, multitudes of laboratory work and X-rays need to be performed. Hospital committees offer instruction to educate the doctors on how to document the medical necessity of the tests and treatments. They are cleverly disguised, not as a way to make more money for the doctor or the hospital, but in how to comply with federal regulations, and make the chart fit for an audit.

Medicare had to find an answer to this because the costs continue to rise: a diagnostic code must accompany the request for a test. For instance, to get a chest X-ray, the code for a cough could be applied. A simple note in the chart about a cough qualifies the test.

I have been the Medical Records Chairman in a local hospital for two decades and I have seen how Medicare changes the rules to pay physicians and hospitals less and less and less. This has spawned efforts from the administrations of hospitals to coach the doctors, nurses, and ancillary people on how to document the chart appropriately to increase the reimbursements. When the rules were changed, exercises were offered in coding classes, in hospitals, books, and so on, to instruct all its providers on how to document the chart and test requisitions so the test would not be denied payment. Medicare complicates its own existence by forcing providers to commit this "legal" fraud. When the auditors come in, they only look for the connections between the requirements for documentation that indicate a medical necessity. It would take a mountain of investigators to root out the documentation fraud that occurs and even then, it would be difficult.

Somewhere this madness has to end. In his speech at the Cleveland City Club, President Bush said that "we have to have as our goal the best medical system in the world." Well, let us start out by saying we *do not*, and that will *not* occur if doctors are bamboozled by hoards of regulations and paid less than hairdressers. Someone has to recognize that if we want the best doctors, we have to pay them what they are worth and allow them to do their jobs under standards they develop themselves.

HOW MEDICARE HAS NEARLY BANKRUPTED HOSPITALS

Let us next look at an example of how Medicare has worked to nearly bankrupt hospitals by cutting reimbursements for standard treatments.

The DRG for the hospital stay for a total knee replacement used to be seven days. This meant that Medicare would reimburse the hospital for a seven-day hospital stay. By mobilizing the patient early and doing early physical therapy, some patients were able to have their hospital stay lowered to three days. This earned four extra days of payment to the hospital for those patients who could be discharged sooner. However, there were many patients, especially the very elderly, who could not be discharged sooner. They had complications more often, so they had to stay in the hospital longer than the seven-day watermark. The payments for the short and long-term patients balanced out. However, when Medicare noticed that a certain percentage of the patients were being discharged sooner, it cut the DRG to fewer days for everyone. This "one size fits all" scheme is not fair to the patients, the doctors, or the hospitals, but "fair" is not in Medicare's list of accepted terms.

This created a huge burden for hospitals. Doctors could get the majority of patients out of the hospital within the new DRG limit, but some were sent home too early because of it. Those patients who developed trouble in the post-op period broke the bank and there was no remedy offered to the hospitals. The hospitals had to eat the cost of the entire time after the DRG expired. It usually cost more to take care of the few patients with complications than they received for the DRG's for routine patients. There was no safety mechanism to help hospitals, but Medicare does not care. In addition, the Medicare officials who make the rules do not suffer with the liability when something goes wrong.

In defense of Medicare and private providers and the problems they face with the high cost in America, hospitals and doctors supported by case managers take advantage of the system. A friend of mine recently brought in a hospital bill her sister had received after being forced to stay in the hospital the last seven weeks of her pregnancy. The bill was $107,000+. For forty-nine days, she had a complete blood count four times a day. Beside each test was a diagnostic code for "anemia." I asked her to get copies of the laboratory work and her "anemia" was an average blood count, 98% of normal. Then I looked at the standard for that hospital and compared it with the three hospitals that I work with, and their standard was higher than any of the hospitals I work with.

Therefore, by just changing the number that kicks out the term ane-mia, the hospital "justified" four blood counts a day. The ethics of this necessarily has to be challenged because the anemia did not change during the entire hospitalization and probably represented what was normal for her sister. Therefore, with a lack of a standard as to what an appropriate number of checks on a patient's blood count should be, the hospital was free to pull the lever. Her sister was given a single 83 mg Aspirin tablet daily under a government-required program for blood clot prevention for a charge of $35 each time she swallowed the tablet. These two examples only represent a drop in the bucket to the mad-ness that took place during her hospitalization. According to the rules of an audit, the hospital passed with flying colors. I can only shake my head when I see things like this happen.

The SGR (Sustainable Growth Rate) formula says the reimburse-ments had to be cut and cut they were. Now hospitals employ teams of people to scour the charts in search of any condition that could in-crease the DRG. For instance, if a patient has a low blood count, the team puts reminders on the chart for the doctor to document that there is an anemia. As witnessed above, different types of anemia are paid differently. The appropriate documentation is coached to the doctor, a simple handwritten entry into the record makes the connection, and the note urging the doctor to make the entry is then conveniently re-moved from the chart.

This has spawned the era of the "case managers" on the wards. People are specifically trained to direct care and move people in and out of the hospital to gain the most from the Medicare DRG and the managed denial insurance companies.

Making rounds in the hospital used to be about checking on the pa-tients and directing what care need be performed. Now, unfortunately, it is at least as important to have daily conferences with the case man-agers in order to terminate care when it looks like there is going to be a cost overrun, or to document the chart to increase reimbursement. All that is well, but it has put the doctor in the liability hot seat because if something adverse happens to the patient, the doctor shoulders the entire liability. Medicare does not care, and, unfortunately, the hospi-tal administrator does not care either, unless the hospital is somehow implicated in the process. This is Economic Survival 101 for hospitals, Medicare, and third party payers. As we can see, the madness contin-ues and there are excesses on both sides that need to be brought under control. But who can be trusted to make it right?

Managed care and senior citizens

There are problems on the patient side, too. I could get into this very deeply, but I am sure everyone who reads this knows someone who is participating in the Medicare entitlement program. Just ask these elderly people about the paperwork. This is disgraceful. The paperwork has one intention, and that is simply to overwhelm people in their senior years when they are tired and many times confused. *It is health care rationing by bureaucratic strangulation.* The idea is simply to smother someone with papers to keep them from seeking health care.

In addition, Medicare has pawned off part of the payment to the newest mega-giant of highway robbery — the managed denial insurance companies. These are the same managed denial insurance companies that are present on the private side. They make money from Medicare by denying treatments they do not want to pay for. Part B costs for the patient have risen so high that they are competing in costs with a regular insurance plan from a managed denial company on the private side.

With the recent entry of managed denial companies partnering with the government, the overall cost to the government has not changed much, but the costs to the patients have increased because they now have to pay co-pays on most things that they did not have to previously. Many of these patients are on fixed incomes, cannot afford the extra charges, and are likely to avoid care; another way Medicare rations health care. In addition, insurance companies have initiated many of the same practices they have been using for years on the private side and defraud patients out of their just care. Recent lawsuits by the government have sought to stop that. The non-medical costs of managing the Medicare program have gone up because now the government has to investigate managed denial companies in addition to all the others. A Part-B plan purchased by the patient to cover the doctor's office, physical therapy, and outpatient services sometimes costs more than a regular insurance plan in the private sector.

I have seen elderly women on fixed incomes with monthly costs of almost $600 per month for Part B coverage alone. For that much money, they could almost buy a standard health insurance plan that would not involve the government madness. In addition, the managed denial company has a say in everything she does. They have instituted the crooked co-pay plan from private insurance that raises the cost to the elderly and results in diminishing the elderly fixed income so much that the patient has to choose between eating and seeking a visit with the doctor.

Managed denial has one intention and that is to discourage people from going to the doctor, and the managed denial insurance companies are very successful at it. Once again, it is health care by financial strangulation. Anathema!

We have not even discussed medications. Until the Bush Administration stepped in and pushed through a Part D Medicare Drug Plan, there was no coverage for most drugs at all. Unfortunately, the new plan still falls far short of what is needed.

Our seniors, for the most part, have lived good lives and have paid loads of taxes to get the entitlements the government has set out for them to protect them in their senior years. Politicians who are in charge of protecting the American people have failed in their jobs miserably. But after we have witnessed the failures of just about everything under their control, is it really surprising that medicine will be the next big institution to fall?

THE NEW PLAN WOULD SOLVE THESE PROBLEMS

Fortunately, something can solve the Medicare dilemma. Not only can the new program provide full and complete care for our seniors, it will take a huge burden off the federal government by eliminating the cost of the Medicare program. We have already shown that seniors are paying nearly as much for Part-B and Part-D coverage in addition to all the new co-pays that were recently introduced. Once the plan is in effect, the government need only collect enough taxes to pay for the premiums for people on the plan. That would be infinitely better than trying to pay for all their health care needs by tax dollars.

Step III's third step would be to bring the entitlement people into the system so that they are treated with the same standards as the rest of the country. They will share in the extreme cost reductions that take place as repetitive, defensive, and entrepreneurial medicine are eliminated, and their premiums are thrown into the pot and left there until needed. In addition, their health care would be controlled by medical standards, not some bureaucrat trying to balance a spreadsheet or a managed denial CEO seeking a huge bonus.

Chapter Thirteen

SUMMARY: HOW THE PLAN WILL WORK

OW THE fun starts. The entire description of our present state of affairs with regard to health care has been penetratingly cast in doom and gloom. There was no bright and rosy way for me to present it to the reader. It is the way it is. The beauty of it all is that there is a real-life solution to this problem. So let us construct the new program from the ground up. No one else has come up with a health care plan on the private side other than managed denial companies who, in their own words, "know some adjustments need to be made but refuse to give up their profits." President Obama has put together a bureaucracy to create a bureaucracy to manage your health care. As a nation, we need to look at all of our options, and this program is attractive for many reasons.

On the government side, President Obama swayed millions of voters with promises to "end the failed policies of the Bush Administration," but after the Medicare fee tug-of-war in the summer of 2008, we can see how out of touch our leaders are with the problems in the system. The Medicare program is too large, too confusing, improperly conceived and administrated, and a downright tragedy for the American people. Our President promised "change we can believe in," but he has demonstrated that he actually wants to continue the failed policies of the Bush Administration. I think we can show him how health care is relatively cheap when managed correctly, as long as government bureaucracy is kept in a cage.

We have just seen the largest expenditure of government funds in the bailout of the real estate and banking industries. Americans are already beginning to question these large expenditures because it is we, after all, who will bear the financial burden. Those government types are living off our money and we are letting them get away with it. Americans are not stupid people, but they are lazy thinkers. One thing they do know, however, is that whenever they have no money left in their checking account, they cannot make it better by continuing to write checks. That one concept will eventually rule all thinking if the Obama Administration tries to institute health care based on tax revenues. There is a much simpler and monumentally cheaper way to bring universal care to Americans and make it work. This bit of sunshine in the midst of all the financial turmoil should be encouraging to all who read this, except perhaps those who favor the Politburo-type government we have had for the past few decades.

So let us make our government an offer they cannot refuse.

LET US CREATE A HEALTH CARE SYSTEM

Before we do anything, however, we need some money. So let us have some fun watching the money come in rather than watching the money go out — by raising taxes.

Insurance companies have ravaged our system of health care and made off with unheard of profits. The news media has had a field day beating up the oil companies for their record profits, but no one has said anything about the profits of the health insurance and medical liability insurance industry; not one word. Exxon, an entire company was all over the news when the whole organization made $10 billion in one quarter. It just slipped by when the CEO of United Health Care took home a $1.74 billion bonus in one year. One person took home a bonus of nearly $2 billion while the news media beat up on Exxon. Then he was reportedly awarded a retirement salary of $5.1 million per year with the option to purchase $2 billion in stock options over the next twenty years. Clearly, the company is cheating you as the patient and cheating your doctor as the provider. They are not just cheating us; it is a financial smack down. His bonus calculates to be more than the total of all the bonuses handed out to AIG, the failing companies in the banking industry, the real estate fiasco, and the automotive crash and no one raised an eyebrow!

LET THE COMPANIES BID FOR THE CONTRACTS

My contention is that we have all the money available to start this program *without* raising taxes. Companies seeking government contracts are supposed to participate in an open bid on the contracts. We have some of the richest companies in the world in our insurance industry. There is nothing wrong with calculating the cost of the initiation of the program, setting the initial bid prices to meet that need, and requiring companies to bid on the right to provide the health insurance in this country.

The concept here is that the small group model is not working to the advantage of the American people. Any attempt to continue the status quo is only going to perpetuate the theft. Therefore, we will eliminate all the cling-ons and reduce our load to a manageable few. Only *three* companies will be allowed to win the bidding contest. It is likely to be three of the largest companies in the business, but not necessarily. Foreign investors could get into the process and make the bidding really explode.

Our minimum bid will be set high enough that some of the companies may not be able to make the mark. Some consolidation will probably have to occur, and I am quite sure they will have to sell stock to get to the minimum, a good old American tried-and-true premise of good business. All this is business as usual in America, so it is a win for America in our present time of financial teetering.

What if some smaller company could borrow the money from China or Japan to make the bid, or what if a foreign entity puts in a bid. This could get interesting. It could be the most fun Americans have had in decades watching these mega-giants of modern highway robbery wallow in the mess they made of their own industry. Losing the bid would mean elimination and certain financial disaster. The employees of the losing companies will not be without work, because the new companies will need plenty of help. If the minimum bid is $50 billion (and in no way do I mean to suggest it should be that small), the three successful bids would bring in a minimum of $150 billion with which to start the company. If a fourth company should survive the initial bidding process, and the four of them have to compete for three available slots, then it could get really interesting.

Mind you now, we are talking about *three hundred million* policies they will get to control. There will be a lot of money in this system to be made, but their profits will be capped by law. Of course, they could borrow money from the government to make the bids, but we need to make sure that doing so will not automatically give the government the right to interfere with health care under any circumstances.

Controls on the Insurance Companies

From recent polls, the American people seem to fear a single payer system. Since all of the universal care systems in the world are single payer type plans, America needs an alternative. What needs to be done is to take the best of both of the types of health care plans we already have and come up with a way that should be acceptable to both sides of the discussion.

This plan calls for only three companies to provide health care for every citizen in the country, including those with private insurance, the reported 47 million uninsured, and those citizens on entitlement programs. The three companies that get the government contract will be chosen through a bidding process. There is good precedent in this country for companies to bid to get government contracts. The initial bid will be set to insure that there will be enough money to begin the program.

The three companies will compete against each other through service to the populace. They cannot enact business plans that try to get medical care for the cheapest price. Medical prices will be established and will not be under control of insurance companies. Their business plans will be restricted to coming up with solutions that seek to better serve the public. The plan that best serves the public will begin to gather greater numbers of policies. That will become the vehicle to allow their profits to accumulate. This style of competition should result in the best service to the public. The model of trying to gouge out the lowest reimbursements to providers has already been proven to adversely affect medical care and will be forbidden.

Profits will be capped at 7%. The days of runaway profits and billion dollar bonuses will come to an end. When profits exceed this level, premiums are reduced to fall within the 0-7% buffer zone. If they fall below zero, premiums will rise to meet the buffer zone. In this way, a company that does well can lower premiums to attract more people. If they perform poorly and have to raise prices to get into the buffer zone, then they could lose policies spurring them to create a better model or fail. Companies that consistently perform poorly over a 3 year period could initiate another bidding process. In this way, we will always have the best companies making it continually easier for our citizens to solve their health care problems.

STEP I — AN ELECTRONIC MEDICAL RECORD

The Obama Administration's answer to an electronic medical record is to spend $10 billion a year for five years to create an electronic medical record. Why reinvent the wheel? As we have seen, online medical records are already in existence and they do not have to be re-created, only expanded and improved upon to fit into the new system. The only thing that needs to be done is to make all the forms and templates uniform between doctors' offices, hospitals, and allied health companies.

No health care provider will be exempt from this system. All hospitals, doctors, and health care providers can have a say-so in the process, but the final decisions will be made by our doctors. The decision-making and liability rests on their shoulders, so they should have the main stake in the creation of the common electronic record, as well as the medical standards that drive the system. Once the common templates are created, the doctors can start immediately to utilize the digital databank.

Over time, the templates can be revised to improve the speed of use and data transfer, but also to increase the quality of care by making the doctor's job easier and more efficient, as well as lowering the cost to patients. As with the standards of care we have talked about so much, the common record will get better and better with time.

READ MY LIPS— NO NEW TAXES

Not one dollar of your tax money has to be spent in creating this system. You have already paid enough over the past four decades as the War on Medicine destroyed your health care system, once the best in the world.

By your actions, this can happen. If you will it to be, it will happen. We are Americans and we can do anything, even create a useful common digital medical record *without raising taxes*.

STEP II — WRITTEN "STANDARDS OF CARE"

This step will be the most difficult because it requires doctors to create the written standards of care they will be practicing. This will be a monumental task because the disagreements in standards will be many, but in the long run, this can and will be managed. In addition, the algorithms they create will have to be fit into the common digital electronic record.

Appropriate charges for the services doctors will perform will be set for everything and no confusing formulas will ever be used again. Everything else in this country has a price tag on it and doctors' services should be no different. Rest assured, there are limits on these, but the intent is to give the profession of medicine a fighting chance to try to attract the best students back into the ranks so that you can benefit from having the best health care once again. This is a good thing! If you are willing to pay Alex Rodriguez $226 million to hit a baseball (after he took steroids to hit it farther), then you should be willing to pay a doctor appropriately to take care of Mr. Rodriguez' injuries that accompany steroid use so he can keep hitting the baseball.

Good pay generally attracts the best of the best and medicine is no different from any other profession. When America's health begins to improve, you should not begrudge your doctor what he or she is earning because the review policies built into the standards will eventually weed out the bad practitioners, and correct or eliminate the things that individual doctors do poorly. With prices established for everything that is done, the only way a doctor can become wealthy is to provide such excellent care that he or she will gather a large practice. That model worked for centuries until our government decided to destroy it.

The standards will control everything. Once you understand this, go back and re-read Barack Obama's health care plan, and try to see if there is one thing that will not be covered by these new written standards. The difference is the consumer and the doctors will control the plan, not the government with its inefficiency, waste, and knee-jerk regulations. This is *your* health care plan, and you will be proud of it as you watch it evolve. This is a good thing for America.

The standards are not written in stone. Every year, every doctor must go into conference to help review and re-write all the standards of care to try to improve the outcomes. Data from years gone by will be used, but the database will involve every patient afflicted with a condition, giving a much more realistic view of how things work. As time goes on, the treatments will get better, mistakes will become fewer in nature and our health care and naturally, our health, will improve. This is our reward for replacing the tired and failing health care policies of today with dynamic care plans that are *self-evolving, self-policing, and self-correcting*. Health care can only get better and cheaper in this way because the big three will be controlled. Liability will be brought under a sensible and realistic control. Repetitive medicine will be eliminated. Doctors will be able to make a good salary without resorting to the types of entrepreneurial escapades that cause our system to suffer. No other plan addresses these issues. Government bureaucracy cannot compete with this model. Managed denial cannot compete with this model. In this time of financial upheaval, is it not refreshing to hear something as positive as this with a real live chance of happening?

STEP III — THE MEDICARE/MEDICAID REVOLUTION

The first two steps actually create the health care plan and initiate the private sector to universal health care. Step III brings the citizens on entitlements into the program. This is particularly inspiring to me for several reasons. The main reason is that our seniors are not getting appropriate health care. They were forced into retirement poverty when Congress was allowed to break into the Social Security Trust Fund. As Medicare stumbled through the last four decades, it just swirled deeper and deeper into failure. As it grew into the mega-giant of failed health care policy it has become, it suffocated all it came into contact with. The bureaucracy has become a dinosaur of decades-old health care policy that is simply failing in all areas it tries to serve.

Furthermore, it is an impediment to the providers trying to do their jobs taking care of those citizens on entitlement programs. The stifling cuts in reimbursement have caused catastrophe amongst our doctor corps. Micromanagement of the doctor-patient relationship has interfered with doctors and nurses doing their jobs, and the morale of both groups has never been poorer. We already have doctor shortages, and we are now faced with a new impending disaster, as half of our doctors have become so frustrated that they are indicating they are going to go do something else. This is not something we can ignore.

In Summary

Health care does not have to be as expensive as it is. Other countries are not going broke paying for it, but the US is. Other countries do not have our liability troubles and their systems are relatively stable and affordable. We should not have to shoulder this national tragedy.

Many people are so desperate that they feel government control is the only thing that will work, but we simply do not have the money to pay for another mega-giant government program. That is what makes this plan so inviting: it not only has the aspects of medical coverage that people think the government will provide, we do not have to raise any taxes to start or maintain the program. In this time of one financial failure after another, this is a bright light in history. With a stable and strong medical policy, America will have one good leg to stand on to begin the reparations that will be needed to keep her as the world's leader.

The retirement of the Medicare and Medicaid programs and replacement of them with a universal health care plan without government control is a happy thought and a welcome relief to all except those that seek to institute the same kind of government in America that we worked decades to defeat. Our citizens want their health care in the hands of their doctors, and with the appropriate controls in the Step III program, this is a prescription for what has been ailing America for decades. There is no better time than the present to make this happen. Americans have had so little to be happy about for so long, this program just has to be the encouragement we need as a nation.

Once the Step III program is in place, all Americans will be able to put health care worries behind them forever. There could not be any better economic or psychological stimulus to our country in our time of turmoil than to stop worrying about health care . . . forever.

CONCLUSION/FINAL WORD

A S A health care professional, I am ashamed of what has happened to my country in regard to access to health care, but I am excited about the possibilities of this plan.

While the small group insurance plan has been wildly successful for investors in and executives of companies, we witness human tragedies occurring every day, as premiums skyrocket, services are eliminated, and medical practices are being destroyed by these mega-giants of modern highway robbery. Part of the American dream is to build a business that becomes successful but not to the extent that it cripples our country and forces families to decide whether they will eat, get health care for their children, or themselves. This is not the America I know and love, and it is not the America I and all of my fellow citizens want to continue. The time has come to release the stranglehold that insurance and government entitlement have on our nation and to bring this national tragedy to a swift and deserved end.

AMERICA HAS A BIG DECISION TO MAKE

President Obama has said he wants health care legislation on his desk before the first of the year 2010. While I am overjoyed to see that someone is finally going to address this national tragedy, I have to worry about how it is going to be implemented. Will we choose socialism or the freedom we all cherish so dearly?

"THE PROBLEM WITH SOCIALISM IS THAT EVENTUALLY YOU RUN OUT OF OTHER PEOPLES' MONEY."

MARGARET THATCHER

In short, in the opinion of this seasoned health care professional, there is no alternative solution to saving the failing program. Socialized medicine simply will not be affordable and maintain the level of care we are used to as a nation. The one-size-fits-all health care of the SPEC's just does not fit in America. Eventually, America *will* run out of other people's money if she keeps on the track she is presently following — it is inevitable.

THE STATISTICS ARE FOR OUR CRITICS

In this book, I have tried to report as much of the story of our recent health care history as I could. The critical statistics should be used for forcing us to take action. One thing that stands out is that this is America! It is not Europe or Asia. This is the greatest country on the earth. We do have the greatest doctors on the planet and we do have the greatest facilities in the world but we also have the worst system of health care in the world.

In the beginning, we did not engage our doctors to assist in the formation of either the government entitlements or the private sector programs. Power and money got in the way. Now we have the opportunity to make it right. We need to turn the best doctors in the world loose to create the best health care plan the world has ever seen. Those that fail to heed the lesson of history are bound to repeat it, and the mistakes of health care in the past should be left in the past.

AT LAST, A WAY TO JOIN HANDS ACROSS THE AISLE

In a press conference, President Obama stated that health care is the anchor that is dragging down the economy. In this plan, he now has a prescription for the future that will not cost one dime of taxes to implement. We will see if his power of fairness and good sense will win out over some desire to see American government change from what our Founding Fathers had in mind and institute something that the likes of Marx, Trotsky, or Lenin had in mind.

President Obama has indicated that he wants to bring the two warring sides of the Congressional aisle together. This health care plan will encourage cooperation between the political right and the political left because it has attractive components to both sides that could set the stage for the historic restoration of the world's best health care system.

With this plan, President Obama should be able to gather the support of the political right who seek to prevent government socialized medicine. By maintaining the American style of competition, which this plan does in a big way, the political right should be satisfied. By making the program universal, the President will accomplish one of his stated goals and satisfy the political left. The political right should enjoy the fact that it is not a government-controlled program, and that it is based on the philosophy that competition in business provides the best model for success, as long as the nation's experts, our doctors, create and maintain appropriate standards of care.

Competition between doctors should be on the basis of the quality of medicine they practice, not to draw business to the one who takes the lowest fee —that is a miserable failure. If the doctor is paid a worthwhile fee for what he does, he can do well for himself if he provides the best service. People will seek out the best doctors. That will be a big step as we try to encourage our best students to return to medicine as a career.

THE MALAISE IN THE DOCTOR CORPS IS SERIOUS

I would caution the young President not to ignore the malaise in the doctor corps that exists. It is real. If not handled correctly, crippling doctor shortages are ahead, as doctors throw up their hands and seek other careers. It will be a monumental task to turn the present dire situation into a success, but our President now has the model that can make that happen.

In the recent SA Opinion, an editorial published on the web at www.mysanantonio.com/opinion/editorials/Needs_of_doctors_crucial, this issue is addressed critically. They state: "The dire diagnosis of the medical profession from those who practice it should be a wake-up call for Congress and other policy makers."

MR. PRESIDENT — PLEASE TRY THIS PLAN AND THEN CALL ME IN THE MORNING

This plan is the health care and political utopia he is seeking as a new President who wants to accomplish great things. With this plan, he can achieve the institution of a universal health care plan and the image that he wants to change in Washington. It is a win-win situation when America is not winning many battles on the home front and uncertainty paints our future.

Based on what he has written in his books, it is not difficult to see that President Obama is an exceptional man, who seems to have the ability to grasp solutions to problems that are not necessarily in the mainstream. I am encouraged to the extent that I believe that he could be the person who *could* grasp onto the concept of this health care plan and actually put it in place. History will record whether he brings real change to health care or more of the same that has already failed.

I watched the White House Health Care Planning Committee and it brought a shiver to my spine. Just what I feared might happen is happening. In the East Room of the White House, a huge conference brought many people to the table to try to come up with a solution to the health care crisis. As I watched each person speak, it became clear that this huge committee was missing the crux of the problem. Everyone there was very erudite and knowledgeable. But they missed the point. A few people skirted the issue, but save for one person, (and who would have thought?) an attorney named Steve Hitov, who is the National Health Law Program Managing Attorney, hit the nail right on the head with a two-ton hammer. He spoke specifically about the interruption of the doctor-patient relationship and no one even noticed. Everyone else in the room had wonderful arguments that their cause was somehow failing, but when examined carefully, the core defect in their cause was the interruption of the doctor-patient relationship in America. This committee represented to me the continuation of the discordant system we have fallen into in our country. They are all on the high ground, and the battle needs to be won in trenches. Once the interruption of the doctor-patient relationship is eliminated, all of their problems will come under control. However, you want to say it: let us not try to sleep while the lights are on; do not miss the forest for the trees; take time to smell the roses or whatever. Please heed the postulates of this writing. I am not fighting for turf like the participants of the health care planning committee. I am just a veteran doctor who offers a cure for what ails America's health care system.

Exceptional wisdom is in order at this time in history, and an old saying paints the picture America needs right now, "If you want to predict the future, then invent it." This health care plan will accomplish that . . . exactly.

The time for real change is now! We must — and we can — win America's War on Medicine!

SELECTED BIBLIOGRAPHY, WORKS CITED, OR SOURCES CONSULTED

The Kaiser Family Foundation is a non-profit, private operating foundation dedicated to providing information and analysis on health care issues to policymakers, the media, the health care community, and the general public. The foundation is not associated with Kaiser Permanente or Kaiser Industries.

The Health Research and Educational Trust is a private, not-for-profit organization involved in research, education, and demonstration programs addressing health management and policy issues. Founded in 1944 as an affiliate of the American Hospital Association, HRET collaborates with health care, government, academic, business, and community organizations across the US to conduct research and disseminate findings that help shape the future of health care.

Health Affairs, *published by Project HOPE, is the leading journal of health policy. The peer-reviewed journal appears bimonthly in print with additional online-only papers published weekly as Health Affairs Web Exclusives at www. healthaffairs.org.*

Andrews, Michelle. America's Best Health Plans. U.S. News & World Report 39;13:48-62. October 10, 2005.

Brown, Lawrence D. The Amazing Noncollapsing U.S. Health Care System – Is Reform finally at Hand? New England Journal of Medicine 358;4:325-327, January 24, 2008

Buchanan, Patrick J. *.Day of Reckoning.* New York. Thomas Dunne Books, St. Martin's Press. 2007.

Conversations and Consultations with David Martin, The Premium Group, Cleveland, Ohio, 2005.

Conversations and Consultations with Robert Trennd, Former President Aetna Eastern States, 2005-2008.

Dobbs, Lou. *Independents Day. Awakening The American Spirit*. New York, NY: Viking, 2007.

Emord, Jonathon W. Murder by Medicare, The Demise of Solo and Small Group Medical Practices. Regulation 21;3:31-39, 1998.

Gingrich, Newt. *Real Change*. Washington DC: Regenery Publishing Co., 2008.

Graph: Will Employers Sustain the inflation? Projected Impact of Healthcare Premium Inflation on Employers. Provided by Robert Trennd, Former President, Aetna Eastern States. Keats, Arthur S. M.D. The ASA Classification of Physical Status-A Recapitulation. Anesthesiology 49: 233-236, 1978.

Kuttner, Robert. Market-Based Failure – A Second Opinion on U.S. Health Care Costs. New England Journal of Medicine. 358;6:549-551, February 7, 2008.

Marx GF, Mateo C.V., Orkin I. R.: Computer analysis of post anesthetic death. Anesthesiology 39: 54-58. 1973. Merritt Hawkins & Associates ®. 2007 Survey of Primary Care Physicians. 1-15.

McQuillan, L.J. and Abramyan, H. March 2008. Pacific Research Institute. Ideas in Action Fact Sheet. U.S. Tort Liability Index: 2008 Report.

Obama, Barack. *The Audacity of Hope*. New York, NY: Crown Publishing, 2006

O'Reilly, Bill. *Culture Warrior*. New York, NY: Broadway Books, 2006.

Owens, WD, Felts JA, Spitznagel EL Jr.: ASA Physical Status Classifications: A study of Consistency of Ratings. Anesthesiology 49;239-243, 1978.

www.expansionmanagement.com. 2005 Health Care Cost Quotient ™. 02/14/2005 by: Michael Keating, Senior Research Editor.

www.kff.org/insurance/ehbs091107nr.cfm. News Release, September 11, 2007. Kaiser/HRET/

www.kff.org/insurance. Kaiser/HRET Survey of Employer-Sponsored Health Plans, Bureau of Labor Statistics 2003 National Compensation Survey.

www.mlo-online.com. Darlene Berger. A brief history of medical diagnosis and the birth of the clinical laboratory. Part 4-Fraud and abuse, managed care and lab consolidation.

www.nchc.org/facts/cost.shtml. National Coalition on Health Care. Health Insurance Costs.

www.usmle.org/Scores_Transcripts/performance/2007.html. 2007 USMLE Performance Data as published in the 2007 NBME Annual Report, Copyright 2008 by the National Board of Medical Examiners®. USMLE Administration, Minimum Passing Scores, and Performance.

A SPECIAL THANK YOU

I COULD NOT end this book without an extra special "thank you" to my editors. I interviewed several people who were recommended to me, but when I communicated with Richard Showstack of Newport Beach, California, I knew immediately that he was the person I wanted to assist me in the publication of this work. My initial impression was that I was about to enter a literary Marine Corps. Immediately, I found myself in the Paris Island of literary works. Once I got to know him, I realized that I really needed someone with his background to guide this publication to print. As he was a former English teacher, I expected to be roughed up about my use of grammar, but I was pleasantly surprised after all these years that I seemed to still have a fairly good hold on that aspect. It was his sense of what belongs where and his constant clarification of my thought processes that have made this book what it has become. I am proud to have met and worked with him.

The final editing was prepared by the fine folks at FirstEditing.com. They provided me the insight on professional writing and added the necessary polish as the manuscript went to print. They are a fine group of people and they turned this project around in what seemed to be record time.

Michael L. Pryce MD

ABOUT THE AUTHOR

D R. PRYCE is an Orthopedic Surgeon who has been in surgical practice for twenty-five plus years.

Prior to beginning college, he spent three years on active duty with the US Navy in Naval Intelligence during the Vietnam War.

In 1973, he graduated from the University of Akron Magna Cum Laude with a degree in Natural Science.

In 1977, he graduated with a Doctor of Medicine from the Bowman Gray School of Medicine at Wake Forest University.

He was admitted to an internship at the Akron City Hospital in a General Surgery program, but shortly afterward, he found his surgical desires lay with the practice of Orthopedic Surgery. The following year, he was admitted into Orthopedic Residency at Akron General Medical Center. Following residency, he was chosen as a Fellow in Hand and Upper Extremity Surgery at Loma Linda University in Loma Linda, California.

During his career, he served in varied posts that brought him close to medical policy decision-making, such as for twelve years as the Department Chairman of Orthopedics and close to twenty years as the Chairman of the Medical Records Committee. He has served on the Senatorial Inner Circle and Presidential Medical Roundtables in Washington, D.C. during the Reagan and Bush Administrations.

He holds an active US Patent for a design of footwear that compensates the common foot deformity of pronated feet (otherwise commonly known as "flat feet"). He started the Marathon Shoe Company that manufactures and markets the FlatFoot® Insole. The insole has solved the problems of countless Americans with conditions, such as "shin splints" and plantar fasciitis. Studies have indicated that the foot-wear offers protection against the dreaded anterior cruciate ligament injury that affects many athletes. It recently received acclaim in an independent study reported in the Wall Street Journal and a scientific study by the Mayo Clinic.

He is also a private pilot in the Single Engine Land Category with Instrument Rating. In addition, he is recently the past President of the Portage County Regional Airport Authority and has been successful in helping bring many improvements to his local airport. He serves in the Airport Support Network, as the local airport volunteer in the Aircraft Owners and Pilots Association (AOPA).

He has been an Amateur Radio Operator since his days in the Navy. He rounds out his experience as an accomplished woodworker, having made many pieces of hardwood furniture in his home.

He resides in Hudson, Ohio with a medical office in Kent, Ohio. He is married to Jo Ellen Pryce, a registered nurse, and the couple has two grown daughters, Meredith and Allison, living and working in New York City.